River Forest

Oak Park →

Where we first met!

Your friend always,

2016

My dear Gerard
Thank you for the
wonderful gift of stories
Much appreciation
— Judy

Gerard -
A wonderful experience
to get to know you and
enjoy your wonderful contributions
to our lives with music
— John & Kathy Solano

Bis Gi
So many memories
and I look forward
to making so many
more.
Evans
Family

Stella, good luck in England!!

Dearest Gerard,
Thank you for beautiful
memories. I'll always cherish
the experience. With love,
Sandra Delgado

From Strauss to
Falla? What a
journey! So wonderful
to have been on it with
you.
Much love,
Heidi & Charlie

Thank you Gerry
Ann Donlyn

Thank you
Don't ever stop
xx3

We wish you
We will miss you -
Bernie + Michelle

[Handwritten inscription, top left:] MCB! Family, I can't express my Thankfulls for your love & kindness. I will see you soon across the pond. Always Hana

[Handwritten inscription, top right:] I feel so blessed to know you Love, Lori J.

[Handwritten inscription, left:] Gerard & Allison: Thank you so much for being fabulous. That can never end. Your friend — Marilyn

HOMETOWN ARCHITECT

THE COMPLETE BUILDINGS OF FRANK LLOYD WRIGHT
IN OAK PARK AND RIVER FOREST, ILLINOIS

PATRICK F. CANNON

WITH AN INTRODUCTION BY PAUL KRUTY
PHOTOGRAPHY BY JAMES CAULFIELD

PRESERVATION TRUST **Frank Lloyd Wright**

Pomegranate

PORTLAND, OREGON

Published by Pomegranate Communications, Inc.
19018 NE Portal Way, Portland OR 97230
800 227 1428; www.pomegranate.com

Pomegranate Europe Ltd.
Unit 1, Heathcote Business Centre
Hurlbutt Road, Warwick
Warwickshire CV34 6TD, UK
[+44] 0 1926 430111; sales@pomeurope.co.uk

All photographs by James Caulfield, unless otherwise noted.

Front cover: Isabel Roberts House (1908; remodeled 1955)
Back cover: Arthur B. Heurtley House (1902)

Library of Congress Cataloging-in-Publication Data
Cannon, Patrick F.
   Hometown architect : the complete buildings of Frank Lloyd Wright in Oak Park and River Forest, Illinois /
by Patrick F. Cannon ; with an introduction by Paul Kruty ; photography by James Caulfield.
      p. cm. — (Pomegrante catalog ; no. A118)
   Includes bibliographical references.
   ISBN 0-7649-3746-4
    1. Wright, Frank Lloyd, 1867–1959—Criticism and interpretation. 2. Architecture, Domestic—Illinois—
History—20th century. 3. Prairie school (Architecture)—Illinois. 4. Oak Park (Ill.)—Buildings, structures, etc.
5. River Forest   (Ill.)—Buildings, structures, etc. I. Wright, Frank Lloyd, 1867–1959. II. Title. III. Series.

NA737.W7C36 2006
720.92—dc22

                                                                        2006043177

Pomegranate Catalog No. A118
ISBN-13: 978-0-7649-3746-0

Cover and book design by Lynn Bell, Monroe Street Studios

Printed in China

22 21 20 19 18 17 16 15 14 13   13 12 11 10 9 8 7 6 5 4

CONTENTS

Frank Lloyd Wright
on the veranda of his
Oak Park home, ca.
1890–1910.
Photograph courtesy
Frank Lloyd Wright
Foundation,
Scottsdale, Arizona.

PREFACE

For the generation that reached maturity in the years after the Second World War, Frank Lloyd Wright was the eloquent, opinionated, eccentric, revered, and maddening grand old man of American architecture. The last great period of his seventy-two-year career coincided with the beginning of the television age, a medium for which he—with his dramatic white hair, flowing capes, porkpie hats, and deep, musical voice—seemed ideally suited.

Like his contemporaries the venerable poets Robert Frost and Carl Sandburg, he was sought out as one who would provide the wisdom of experience, whether extolling the virtues of his mile-high skyscraper for Chicago, jousting during an interview with the young Mike Wallace, or pointing out the "sins" of the International Style during a stroll in Manhattan. When he died in 1959, it was this image—a venerable sage who still looked to the future—that remained.

But we should remember that Wright was born in 1867, only two years after the end of the Civil War, and that his ideas were rooted in the ideals of the nineteenth century. While he embraced new building technologies throughout his career, his bedrock philosophy never seemed to stray very far from the visions of Jefferson, Emerson, and Lincoln,

visions that valued individual rights, self-reliance, and non-intrusive government. As a very young man, he had tried to adapt older European forms to new uses, but within ten years of starting his career he began to abandon them entirely in favor of a new, purely American, and—as he would call it—democratic architecture.

This book covers approximately the first twenty years of Wright's career, when he developed the first of his American architectures, what has come to be known as the Prairie style. It concentrates on the houses and buildings the younger Wright built for his friends and neighbors in Oak Park and River Forest, Illinois, adjoining villages to the west of Chicago that contain the largest surviving concentration of his work. The first house he designed in Oak Park was the first house he ever designed. Built in 1889 for himself and his new wife, Catherine Tobin Wright, it was a modest example of the popular Queen Anne/Shingle-style houses of the period, influenced by such well-known architects as Henry Hobson Richardson, Bruce Price, and Wright's first employer, Joseph Lyman Silsbee. The last house he designed for Oak Park, the Adams House of 1913—when he was still only forty-six—was one of the last Prairie houses, built as he was beginning to move toward new forms, a process of reinvention that he continued throughout his long life.

This book explores not only the buildings he designed for Oak Park and River Forest, but also the people for whom he designed them. For an architect, the first step is securing the client, and Wright was fortunate in finding men and women who were willing to travel with him on the sometimes rocky road to a new architecture. Most of his clients belonged to what we would now call the upper middle class. They included doctors, lawyers, manufacturers, wholesalers, inventors, publishers, stockbrokers, and bankers. Although few were university graduates, most were well read, with an interest in literature and the arts. Their religion was Protestant, but often of a liberal cast. Many were Unitarians and would have admired Wright's preacher uncle, Jenkin Lloyd Jones, who was nationally known and whose Chicago church had been designed by Joseph Lyman Silsbee. Unlike the truly rich, who preferred a more conservative architecture, they were willing to give their young neighbor a chance.

While Wright could be difficult to work with, he nevertheless managed to establish lasting friendships with many of his clients. This led in many cases to new and more lucrative commissions over the years. Whatever the difficulties with which he confronted his clients, they were almost always overcome by his legendary charm and their recognition of his obvious genius. He was nothing if not a social man and never lost his ability to stimulate both individuals and groups.

I have been giving tours of these buildings for some thirty years, under the auspices of the Frank Lloyd Wright Preservation Trust. I regularly encounter people who are struck by the "newness" of the later houses, many of which are now more than one hundred years old and still surrounded by their more conventional contemporaries. Others walk past the early "bootleg" houses without recognizing them as Wright's work. But whether a building represents the young Wright's take on the Queen Anne or Tudor styles, the influence of his mentor Louis Sullivan, or his own appreciation of the Japanese aesthetic, each is part of the larger story of Wright's development as an artist.

We are fortunate that most of the buildings that he designed for Oak Park and River Forest still survive, and that most have undergone, or are undergoing, restoration. All lovers of Wright's architecture thus owe a great debt of gratitude to their dedicated owners. For demolished or never-built projects, or where certain features of surviving buildings have been lost or changed, we have included period photographs or illustrations. Whether new or old, the photographs help tell the full story of Oak Park and River Forest's hometown architect.

—Patrick F. Cannon
Oak Park, Illinois

A Note on the Prairie Style

Throughout this book, the term *Prairie* is used to describe the style of homes Wright designed in the years 1900 to 1918. During the 1890s, he had moved toward what he called a new American architecture, one that was appropriate to the needs of the people and landscape of the prairie Midwest. It rejected the add-on decorative motifs of historical models in favor of a more organic and intrinsic decoration, and the use of simple, more natural materials. Because Wright—who grew up in southern Wisconsin and moved to largely flat Chicago when he was nineteen—believed his native landscape demanded low proportions, a horizontal line dominates most of his Prairie-house designs. A typical Wright Prairie house has a low hipped or flat roof with wide, sheltering eaves; long bands of art-glass windows; banded wooden, concrete, or stone trim; and a pronounced water table to anchor the building firmly to its site. Inside, the floor plan is open, radiating outward from a central fireplace. Furnishings are not secondary elements but integral to the design, and hence often consist of built-ins. In this book, the Thomas, Heurtley, Laura Gale, and Adams Houses represent excellent examples of the type.

Another often-used term is *Prairie School,* which describes a group of architects and landscape designers who followed Louis Sullivan (1856–1924) but were influenced also by Wright's forms and ideas. Many of them—John Van Bergen (1885–1969), William Drummond (1876–1946), Barry Byrne (1883–1967), and Walter Burley Griffin (1876–1937), among others—worked for Wright early in their careers and went on to make their own significant contributions.

■

ACKNOWLEDGMENTS

In addition to the generous owners of Frank Lloyd Wright buildings, many people helped me in the preparation of this book. Joan B. Mercuri, president and CEO of the Frank Lloyd Wright Preservation Trust, and Zarine Weil, senior publications manager, concurred that my idea for the book might be a good one; both have helped and supported me from the beginning. Zarine additionally has served as my editor, to my great benefit. Longtime Preservation Trust volunteer Jack Lesniak, AIA, also reviewed the text and made numerous helpful suggestions. In addition to writing the excellent introduction, Paul Kruty, professor of architecture at the University of Illinois at Urbana-Champaign, made many useful recommendations for the text. Any errors that remain are my responsibility alone. I am also indebted to Valerie Harris, the Preservation Trust's librarian and archivist, and to her assistant, Rebecca Hyman, for their help in supplying research materials and acquiring historical photographs. In this regard, I am also grateful to William Jerousek of the Oak Park Public Library, and Frank Lipo and Diane Hansen of the Historical Society of Oak Park and River Forest. Nor could the book have been done without the voluminous research carried out over many years by Preservation Trust volunteers, usually in support of the organization's annual Wright Plus house walk. They have learned far more details about Wright's buildings than I could use in this book; their research is a unique and valuable resource for anyone interested in Wright's work in Oak Park and River Forest. Finally, one of the great pleasures of writing this book was the opportunity to work with photographer Jim Caulfield and his assistant, Tim Walters. An illustrated book on architecture can succeed only if its photographs are worthy of the subject. In this case, as you will see, they are.

■

INTRODUCTION
FRANK LLOYD WRIGHT AND OAK PARK

PAUL KRUTY

Frank Lloyd Wright and Oak Park, Illinois, are inextricably entwined. If Madison, Wisconsin, held an emotional place in Wright's heart as his point of departure,[1] Oak Park was where he actually lived during the crucial decades when he first envisioned a new architecture that was both American and modern. It is also the site of the studio where this vision was turned into sketches and working drawings by a remarkable collection of talented associates. And Oak Park, along with its closely linked western neighbor, River Forest, is the location of a surprising number of the buildings constructed from these ideas and plans over the course of a quarter century. Following this first "Golden Age," Wright worked for the next fifty years far removed from Chicago's western suburbs. But long after scholars began sorting out just what did and did not happen here, individuals and institutions in Oak Park and River Forest have continued to restore the architecture and promote Wright's charismatic persona, while his buildings have made the quiet suburb an international travel destination.

Wright's Oak Park years, spent during his twenties and thirties, fascinate us as do no others. His Prairie style, universally admired for its sheer brilliance, is seen by many as a rich new architecture analogous to the contemporary creations of Charles Rennie Mackintosh, C. F. A. Voysey, Joseph Maria Olbrich, and a host of Wright's international colleagues who sought to express what has been called "the cultural high-bourgeois dwelling in its own ground."[2] Unlike these contemporaries, Wright survived the cataclysm of World War I with his career intact, eventually to assume his role as "the world's most famous architect."

Wright's neighbors saw him somewhat differently, as he changed from a young newlywed drafting for the big Chicago firm of skyscraper architects, Adler & Sullivan, into a father of six and a prominent, if eccentric, local figure. They watched him become a successful domestic architect, whose characteristic work—and increasingly that of his followers— seemed to spring up overnight on every other street corner.[3] Yet to locals, Wright was akin to a small-town architect who catered to their whims and needs. He provided mansions for native pooh-bahs, like industrialist William Winslow, lawyer Nathan Moore, and judge Jesse Baldwin.[4] He agreed to remodel the houses of his neighbors, the Youngs, Robertses, Wallers, Hills, Beachys, and Copelands. He worked with local developers, including Charles Roberts and E. C.

Waller, and designed shops for Main Street businesses like Cummings real estate and Pebbles & Balch decorators. He attended Unity Temple, the Unitarian church in town, many of whose parishioners numbered among his clients and whose new building he eventually planned. He designed and printed books by hand in the fashionable Arts and Crafts manner with two of his local clients, W. H. Winslow and Chauncey Williams. And he socialized with a number of his professional colleagues who lived nearby, including the architect Robert C. Spencer Jr. and the sculptor Richard Bock.

It makes perfect sense that Wright acquired a large lot, with an existing house for his mother and plenty of room for his own house, in a burgeoning suburb that was mere minutes away from Chicago's commercial core yet still practically rural. By settling in Oak Park in 1889, Wright also staked his claim to the west side of the great metropolis, neatly navigating between two of the brightest architectural stars in the regional firmament: Daniel H. Burnham (1846–1912), who lived up north in Evanston, and Louis H. Sullivan (1856–1924), who could be found to the south in Hyde Park.

Following the lead of America's most famous architect during his teenage years, Henry Hobson Richardson (1838–1886), Wright longed to build a working studio next to his residence, as Richardson had done in Brookline, Massachusetts, in 1881. In 1898, Wright accomplished this goal. In contrast to virtually every other suburban professional, including all his clients, the architect no longer commuted to Chicago's Loop, where he kept only a business address. In Oak Park, he continued to collect talented associates. He already employed Marion Mahony (1871–1961), who was widely traveled and a Unitarian like Wright, with a professional architecture degree from Massachusetts Institute of Technology. At the Studio she was joined by William Drummond (1876–1946) in 1899 and Walter Burley Griffin (1876–1937) in 1901, both of whom had studied architecture at the University of Illinois. By late 1901, all three had passed the Illinois architects' licensing exam, something not normally done by the drafting staff. Four licensed architects, including Wright, in a small suburban office: this was truly unusual. It meant that during the years that saw the creation of the Thomas, Fricke, Heurtley, and Cheney Houses, Wright had one of the most professional small-scale residential practices in the Chicago area.[5] Artists, sculptors, and decorators routinely dropped by to discuss the latest work.[6]

This manner of creative surroundings is exactly what Wright needed and wanted during the first years of the Oak Park Studio. Far from wishing to work in a vacuum, removed from architectural developments around him, Wright wanted to know everything, sometimes testing a motif or method he had discovered in another architect's work on his own buildings. More often, he discussed the idea, if not its source, with Mahony, Drummond, or, most especially, Griffin. Particularly when Wright was in the midst of a creative dilemma, he bounced his thoughts off his red-haired colleague. He also came to rely on Griffin's ability to solve the problem of actually constructing his dreams.

In this sense, Wright's built work is very much the result of collaboration. Evidence of diverse joint undertakings abounds in the Oak Park buildings. There are the more traditional additions of sculpture and painting to architecture, as when artists Charles Corwin, Orlando Gianinni, and Pauline Dohn added murals to Wright's own house and the houses of Chauncey Williams and Charles Roberts, or when Richard Bock worked on the Studio. Intra-office collaborations are also to be found, if you know where to look for them. Among Griffin's first responses to Wright's work when he joined the staff was to suggest that the dining room of the Thomas House be turned ninety degrees to face the street and block the view to the Romanesque row houses to the south, producing one of the nicest urban configurations on Forest Avenue. This sensitivity to context, something for which Wright eventually developed a sixth sense, was, in 1901, as underdeveloped in Wright as it was natural for Griffin. Among many other examples, Marion Mahony's entrance panels still face the Studio visitor, while numerous staff decisions (probably including Mahony's) grace the nearby Beachy House of 1906.

Collaboration of a different sort continued to affect Wright's Oak Park buildings after these architects left his employ and after Wright himself left the suburb altogether. For example, Griffin landscaped the William Martin House in 1909. Similarly, Charles E. White enlarged the Charles E. Roberts House a number of times. Tallmadge & Watson, perhaps with the assistance of White, provided a sympathetic addition to the Thomas House, while William Drummond remodeled the Isabel Roberts House.

Collaboration even extended to finding commissions. When potential clients rang the bell and Mr. Wright was out, staff members often explained the work effectively on their own. Marion Mahony recalled a day in September 1902 when "only Walt [Griffin] was in the office when he saw that a car had stopped in front."[7] It was William Martin and his brother Darwin. Griffin invited them in and he, not Wright, advocated the value of Wright's work. As Darwin wrote to Elbert Hubbard immediately after, "To my uncultivated mind, Mr. Wright's houses . . . seemed very fancy, but after I had a talk with Mr. Wright's Red One [Griffin], I was convinced that the style is simplicity itself."[8] Griffin argued that these seemingly complicated and costly buildings were, in fact, practical and economical. The interview led not only to the William Martin House in Oak Park, but to the Larkin Building and four more houses in Buffalo, New York.

Frank Lloyd Wright, of course, was more than a home-town architect with talented help. The work created during his Oak Park years radically altered the course of twentieth-century architecture. When he arrived in the suburb, Wright was a skillful designer of picturesque, Shingle-style buildings, a manner of design learned from his first employer, Joseph L. Silsbee. Attention to materials and unexpected encounters and views characterize his own house of 1889 as well as the "bootlegged" works of the early 1890s, including frame houses for the Gale brothers, Robert Parker, and Francis Woolley. Wright would soon respond profoundly to the ideas of Louis Sullivan, his employer, mentor, and model, who instilled in his young protégé the burning desire to express contemporary culture through a new personal architecture. Wright's first such response, the Winslow House of 1894, combines Sullivan's formality and modern ornament with a picturesque rear stair tower and entryway inglenook that Sullivan would never have sanctioned, while adding a central fireplace and massive, hovering hipped roof that are all Wright's own.

Wright struggled mightily during the 1890s to find his way to his self-imposed goal. He experimented with historic styles, such as Tudor Gothic for the Moore House, and combined Silsbee and Sullivan in exotic ways for the Williams House. At the end of the decade, he focused his attention on a more limited range of ideas in a series of masonry buildings, including the two Furbeck Houses, the Winslow stable, and the Studio addition. Then, for the River Forest Golf Club, a frame building designed early in 1899 but unfortunately demolished, Wright first covered an entire complex composition with a single overhanging hipped roof at one level.

He began to find his own voice in 1900, producing the combination of forms that we now call his Prairie style. But he continued to experiment with these elements through 1902, as is evident in the very different results found in the Thomas, Davenport, Fricke, and Martin Houses. Three of them use Wright's new preferred material, plaster over frame, while the more modest Davenport House was sheathed in lap siding. The Thomas House reveals Wright's preference, where possible, for elevating the main living spaces to the second floor. The towering Fricke and Martin Houses show that horizontality was not an immutable feature in early Prairie houses.

Wright's presence in the suburban village continued for another decade. The early 1900s saw the construction of two of the greatest Prairie houses, for banker Arthur Heurtley and his wife, Grace, and lawyer Edwin Cheney and his wife, Mamah. Decade's end witnessed two of the later Prairie types, for Isabel Roberts and Laura Gale. In the midst of the Studio years, Wright created Unity Temple, with its severe geometry of interlocking forms. If the concrete building gave pause to locals, it was destined to become one of the iconic works of the twentieth century.

Early in the next decade, Wright received commissions for houses from Oscar Balch and Harry Adams, both built between Wright's move to Wisconsin in 1911 and the devastating tragedy of the Taliesin fire and murders in 1914, which effectively ended his years as a Midwestern architect. Henceforth, he returned to the Oak Park area on a professional basis only to reconstruct the Moore House following its disastrous fire in 1923 and to remodel the Roberts House in 1955.

For those seeking to understand the accomplishments of Frank Lloyd Wright, Oak Park and River Forest remain the ideal textbook. This ensemble of work is without parallel, and it allows us to trace Wright's development as an architect. On the village streets, the story unfolds before our eyes. May the collection of observations and photographs that follow serve as your introduction to many happy hours of wandering and learning.

■

1 See M. J. Hamilton, "Frank Lloyd Wright's Madison Networks," in P. E. Sprague, ed., *Frank Lloyd Wright and Madison: Eight Decades of Artistic and Social Interaction* (Madison, WI: Elvehjem Museum of Art, 1990), 1.

2 Reyner Banham, "Death and Life of the Prairie School," *Architectural Review* 154 (August 1973): 99. Banham similarly called this the "the Arts & Crafts villa movement."

3 For a helpful overview of Wright and the Prairie School in Oak Park, as well as the general significance of the movement, see Paul E. Sprague, *Guide to Frank Lloyd Wright and Prairie School Architecture in Oak Park,* 5th ed. (Oak Park, IL: Oak Park Landmarks Commission, 1986).

4 The intended location of the Baldwin House at 323 N. Kenilworth—just east of the Heurtley house—was first determined and published in Paul Kruty, *Prelude to the Prairie Style: Eight Models of Unbuilt Houses by Frank Lloyd Wright, 1893–1901* (Urbana, IL: University of Illinois School of Architecture, 2005).

5 For biographies of the Studio staff, see Fran Martone, *In Wright's Shadow: Artists and Architects at the Oak Park Studio* (Oak Park, IL: Frank Lloyd Wright Home and Studio Foundation, 1998). For an account of Studio practice, including the situation after Griffin left in 1906, see Paul Kruty, "At Work in the Oak Park Studio," *Arris* 14 (2003): 17–32.

6 Charles E. White Jr., who worked for Wright briefly, has left an engaging account of these activities in a series of letters; see Nancy K. Morris Smith, ed., "Letters, 1903–1906, by Charles E. White, Jr., from the Studio of Frank Lloyd Wright," *Journal of Architectural Education* 25 (Fall 1971): 104–112.

7 Marion Mahony Griffin to William Gray Purcell, c. 1947, William Gray Purcell Papers, Northwest Architectural Archives, University of Minnesota, Minneapolis.

8 Darwin Martin to Elbert Hubbard, September 19, 1902, Martin Correspondence, State University of New York, Buffalo.

The FRANK LLOYD WRIGHT HOME AND STUDIO was the incubator for an American architecture. This is the north façade showing the Studio complex. The gable in view behind the studio is part of the Home; behind the windows is the master bedroom.

FRANK LLOYD WRIGHT HOME AND STUDIO

HOME 1889. STUDIO 1898

1

The first house that Frank Lloyd Wright designed was his own Oak Park home, now part of what is known as the Frank Lloyd Wright Home and Studio. As built in 1889, the modest structure included six rooms: living, dining, kitchen, two bedrooms, and an architect's studio. The house was built near the west end of a lot at the corner of Forest and Chicago avenues that already had a small Gothic cottage to the east, facing Chicago Avenue. His mother, Anna, and sister Maginel occupied the existing house, which now serves as the offices of the Frank Lloyd Wright Preservation Trust.

Newly married to Catherine Tobin, Wright borrowed the five thousand dollars he needed for the property from his employer, Louis Sullivan, to be paid back by deductions from his paycheck. The house was built in the fashionable Shingle style and may have been modeled most closely after the 1886 Chandler House in Tuxedo Park, New York, designed by Bruce Price (1845–1903). Wright's former employer, Joseph Lyman Silsbee (1848–1913), also designed in the Shingle style, as did America's most famous architect of the time, Henry Hobson Richardson (1838–1886).

The Wrights had six children between 1890 and 1903, with four arriving by 1895. The family was clearly outgrowing the house, so major changes and additions were made in 1895. A seven-foot wall was installed in the former studio to create separate bedrooms for boys and girls. The first-floor kitchen and a nursery above were expanded by the addition of a large bay, the kitchen becoming a new, larger dining room, and the nursery a pleasant dayroom for Catherine. A separate addition provided a new kitchen and servant's room on the first floor; above it, Wright created a magical, barrel-vaulted playroom.

Wright began his practice in 1893 after being fired by Louis Sullivan for accepting independent commissions. He initially rented office space in the Sullivan-designed Schiller Building, perhaps because he had himself worked on its design. Until he lost his in-home studio in 1895, he worked both in his city office and at home. In 1898, in an effort to return to a closer work-family relationship and in response to a growing practice, he decided to build a new studio adjacent to his home, connected by a passageway. Both would serve as laboratories for his emerging style, as he constantly remodeled them to try out new ideas.

Built facing Chicago Avenue, a major arterial street that runs through both Oak Park and Chicago, the Studio uses the same materials as the Home (shingles, common brick, concrete, and wood trim) but in a form clearly meant to impress prospective clients. It has a binuclear plan, with an entrance lobby serving a large drafting room, library, and office. Although different in terms of scale and materials, Unity Temple in Oak Park uses a similar plan, which Wright defined as two separated structures joined by a common lobby. The drafting room and library are octagons, a shape that Wright used many times, including in the nearly contemporaneous George Furbeck House, also in Oak Park.

Wright went to Europe in 1909 with his mistress, Mamah Cheney, whom he had met when he designed a house for her and her husband, Edwin, in 1903. After leaving Oak Park for Wisconsin permanently in 1911, he converted the Studio into living space for his family, the original home providing rental income for them. He added a garage that served both units, with an additional rental unit above. As late as 1956, Wright returned to do some remodeling.

When the Frank Lloyd Wright Home and Studio Foundation (now the Frank Lloyd Wright Preservation Trust) embarked on the property's restoration in 1974, their task was complicated by the fact that the complex had been carved into as many as six separate living units during the housing shortage of World War II. It took thirteen years, painstaking research, considerable volunteer labor, and nearly three million dollars to return the Home and Studio to the way it looked when Wright left for Europe in 1909.

■

The Frank Lloyd Wright Home and Studio is open to the public. For information about tours and other programs, visit www.wrightplus.org or call 1-708-848-1976.

A view of the living room, looking northwest. The bay to the left was part of the original house; Wright added the second bay when he made other alterations in 1895. The chairs are an early Wright take on the famous Morris chair, although the version sold by William Morris had an adjustable back. Most of Wright's furniture during the Prairie period was based on Arts and Crafts models, including the print table seen here. Visitors are often surprised to find classical detailing like the coffered ceiling and dentil molding. Photographer: Jon Miller, Hedrich Blessing Photographers.

The dining room was created in 1895 by adding a bay to the space that had originally been the kitchen. The laylight grille, with its pattern of oak leaves and complicated geometric forms, shows Louis Sullivan's influence. The table and chairs are original. Photographer: Tim Long. © Frank Lloyd Wright Preservation Trust.

The playroom is among Wright's most famous early spaces. The four curved ceiling grilles, this time combining geometry with stylized prickly ash leaves, let in natural light from the skylight above. The art-glass light fixtures and tulip-themed bay windows were not part of the space when it was first designed in 1895 but were added later by an architect who constantly changed features in both his home and studio. The photograph is taken from the balcony, which seems largely decorative but was a magical space to Wright's children. Photographer: Tim Long. © Frank Lloyd Wright Preservation Trust.

Wright built his Studio in 1898, paying for it—he later wrote—with money he earned designing glass prisms and sample building designs using them, for the American Luxfer Prism Company, whose part owners were his friends and clients Edward Waller and William Winslow. The chain harness helps hold the structure together against the pressure of the ceiling beams. Separate chains support the balcony and then continue down to support the glass globes that provide general illumination. The drafting tables and cabinets are reproductions of the originals. Photographer: Jon Miller, Hedrich Blessing Photographers.

The Studio reception area was clearly meant to impress visitors and prospective clients, with its gold walls, rich trim, and colorful skylights. The stork capitals from the exterior loggia are visible through the windows behind the large plan desk, placed here so contractors and others could review plans without disturbing workers in the drafting room. Photographer: Jon Miller, Hedrich Blessing Photographers.

The THOMAS H. GALE HOUSE is more angular than the typical Queen Anne house of the period.

THOMAS H. GALE HOUSE 1892
ROBERT P. PARKER HOUSE 1892
WALTER GALE HOUSE 1893
FRANCIS J. WOOLLEY HOUSE 1893

2

In his *Autobiography,* Frank Lloyd Wright describes how he came to leave Adler & Sullivan in 1893. As with many turning points in his life, only his version of the event survives. "I threw my pencil down," he wrote, "and walked out of the Adler & Sullivan office never to return."

Before throwing the pencil, he had a confrontation with Louis Sullivan regarding some houses he had designed "out of office hours." His contract with the firm did not permit him to design anything on his own account, although he claimed he was ignorant of this clause. Wright had likely succeeded in paying back the five thousand dollars he had borrowed from his employer to build his own home in Oak Park and felt ready to assert his independence. The irony is that he probably would not have been able to retire his debt had he not designed what have come to be known as the "bootleg" houses.

In the block immediately west of his own home are two of the houses that Sullivan objected to: the Thomas H. Gale and Robert P. Parker Houses, both commissioned by Gale and built in 1892. In 1893, after leaving Adler & Sullivan, Wright added a third house to the block, built for Thomas Gale's older brother, Walter. It was Wright's first independent commission.

The Gales belonged to one of Oak Park's founding families. Their father, Edwin O. Gale, had moved to the Chicago area from New York in the 1830s. Among his real estate holdings was the land upon which Unity Temple was later built. Thomas, just a year older than Wright, was a lawyer and real estate developer who shared membership with him in Oak Park's Universalist Church. As so often happened with Wright, the relationship proved to be long lasting and productive. In 1897, he designed a summer cottage in Michigan for Thomas and his wife, Laura. Following Thomas' premature death in 1907, he designed another house for Laura in Oak Park (see pages 113–115). Finally, he designed three rental cottages in the Prairie style for her summer property in Michigan. The Michigan cottages still exist, although they have been winterized and otherwise updated.

Walter Gale, several years older than Thomas, was a partner in a small chain of drugstores his father had started with William Blocki. He had the distinction of being in the first graduating class of what is now Oak Park and River Forest High School. While he knew Wright as a fellow member of the Universalist Church, Wright's close friendship with his brother likely led him to choose the young architect to design his own home. Unlike Thomas and his wife, Walter chose another architect, E. E. Roberts, when he decided to build a larger, Colonial Revival house in 1906.

As he intended, Thomas Gale sold one of the lots before construction even began to Robert P. Parker, an attorney who was shortly to be married. Parker, born in Vermont in 1860, moved to Chicago with his family in 1863. He attended Lakeview High School and Lake Forest College before graduating from Dartmouth College in 1882, and played baseball for the Chicago White Stockings (now the Cubs) from 1878 to 1880.

When built, the Thomas Gale and Robert Parker Houses were nearly identical and very similar to the Emmond House in LaGrange, Illinois, also from 1892. The Walter Gale House is larger and more elaborate, but all three are in the popular Queen Anne style, favored by Wright's former employer, Joseph Lyman Silsbee.

Although Wright later dismissed some of his early houses as being done primarily to pay the bills, he nevertheless put his unique stamp on them. The Thomas Gale and Parker houses are highly geometric and linear, with octagonal bays and extremely generous windows. Both have been restored in recent years, but only the Parker has had its original side porch reconstructed.

Across the backyard from the Parker House is perhaps one of Wright's most conventional Queen Anne houses, built for attorney Francis J. Woolley in 1893.

■

The ROBERT P. PARKER HOUSE had its well-integrated side porch reconstructed during a recent restoration.

T. H. GALE, PARKER, W. GALE, AND WOOLLEY HOUSES

The WALTER GALE HOUSE—built on the existing foundation of a house originally designed by Solon S. Beman (1853–1914)—has a prominent circular turret bay, a two-story dormer with a decorative spandrel, and an unusual (for the time) open veranda instead of the typical covered porch. It also includes a sheltered, somewhat hidden, side door. In his later Prairie houses, Wright would challenge visitors to find his ingeniously hidden entrances.

The FRANCIS J. WOOLLEY HOUSE, one of Wright's most conventional Queen Anne designs, lies just across the backyard from the Parker House. Unlike the other houses, it has ordinary double-hung windows and a traditional front porch. For many years, it had been sided with asphalt shingles but has now been returned to its original clapboard-and-shingle siding. Many of Wright's original interior features were removed.

On the second floor of the Walter Gale House, the windows of the circular turret provide abundant north light for a home office.

Morning light streams into the Parker House dining room through unusually generous windows. The wall and ceiling colors are based on surfaces uncovered during restoration. Wright designed the table runner in the 1950s for F. Schumacher & Company.

The WILLIAM H. WINSLOW HOUSE has been described as the precursor to the later Prairie houses. With them, it shares a hipped roof with wide, sheltering eaves, low chimney, and bold water table, with no suggestion of a basement below (although there is one).

WILLIAM H. WINSLOW HOUSE

3

1894

In William H. Winslow, Frank Lloyd Wright found a heaven-sent client: a man with money who was willing to give a young architect some creative license.

When Winslow commissioned Wright to build his River Forest house in 1894, he was, at thirty-six, already a highly successful businessman. His company provided ornamental iron and bronze to many architects, including Adler & Sullivan, Wright's employer until the spring of 1893. Architectural metals were a feature of most important commercial buildings of the time, used for such things as exterior ornament, elevator doors and grilles, and railings of various kinds. Louis Sullivan made lavish use of these features, as in the 1893 Chicago Stock Exchange building. As chief draftsman for Adler & Sullivan, Wright would have been involved in working with suppliers like Winslow, and this is undoubtedly how they met.

As their friendship developed, they discovered many shared interests, including music, photography, and technical innovation. One of Winslow's other interests was printing, and Wright later collaborated with him and a future client, Chauncey Williams, in producing hand-printed books—

prepared and produced in the Winslow House and stables— which Wright designed and embellished. Published under the imprint of the Auvergne Press (named after the street where the Winslow House stands), one of the titles was Unitarian minister William C. Gannett's *House Beautiful,* which extolled many of the features of domestic architecture that Wright also espoused.

The house was built on property that was part of the Edward Waller estate, as was the house that Wright designed for Chauncey Williams in 1895. Wright's productive association with Waller likely began as he was building Winslow's house. This led to work on Waller's own estate— house remodeling, poultry house, stables, and ornamental gates (see page 138 in the chapter on lost and altered structures)—along with several apartment buildings and some unbuilt projects, including an amusement park at Wolf Lake on the far southeast side of Chicago. For Waller's son, Edward Jr., Wright designed the famous Midway Gardens (1913, demolished 1929).

Winslow's house faced Waller's. For many years, the land surrounding the Winslow House on the other sides was largely vacant. Such environs would have supported Wright's later claim that the Winslow was his first Prairie house. It is now surrounded by suburban development.

Unlike the later Prairie houses, the Winslow has a formal, almost classical, façade. The front door, surrounded by a decorated stone frame, has a foliate panel clearly derivative of Sullivan, as is the textured plaster frieze—originally a lighter brown—that defines the second floor. Below this, Wright used one of his favorite materials, Roman brick. The large double-hung windows are precisely placed. In contrast to this formality, Wright later took pains to hide his entries and used long bands of casement windows that he called "light screens." Elements like the porte cochere were also better integrated into the main structure, and later interior plans opened up the space to provide for free circulation.

Nevertheless, the Winslow stands proudly today as Wright's first great house. He certainly had reason to thank Winslow for the opportunity, for as he himself wrote in his *Autobiography,* "The Winslow House had burst on the view of that provincial suburb like the Prima Vera in full bloom. It was a new world to Oak Park and River Forest. That house became an attraction far and near. Incessantly it was courted and admired. Ridiculed too of course."

In contrast to the formality of the front, the rear façade includes a circular bay and an octagonal stair tower whose windows are decorated with Gothic tracery. Along with the stable, it more clearly points to Wright's Prairie future than does the front façade.

34
WILLIAM H. WINSLOW HOUSE

Above: Although the Waller estate is long gone, part of the gates that Wright designed for it still mark the entrance to Auvergne Place and the Winslow House. The gates were partially restored in the late 1980s, when the stone pylons were repaired and the lanterns rewired. Swinging gates are still missing from the auto and pedestrian entrances.

Above left: Directly facing the front door, the fireplace sits at the physical and emotional center of the house. Two steps above the entry hall, its inglenook is entered through an arcade whose slender columns are topped by intricately carved capitals and pediments. With its built-in benches, it is clearly meant as a gathering place.

Below left: The dining room bay, with its shimmering art-glass windows and built-in seating, seems also meant as a gathering place. One can imagine guests relaxing there after dinner. The columns on each side have less formal, foliate capitals. The bay was once separated from the main dining area by low built-in cabinets.

The NATHAN G. MOORE HOUSE may be Wright's most eclectic design. It combines elements of the Prairie and Tudor, and the architect's early-1920s California Romanza styles.

NATHAN G. MOORE HOUSE

1895. REBUILT AFTER FIRE. 1923

4

Wright's prospective client Nathan Moore was born in Pennsylvania in 1853. A graduate of Lafayette College, he moved to La Crosse, Wisconsin, and opened a music store. He then began studying law and was admitted to the bar in 1877, after having moved to Peoria, Illinois. There he met Anna Walker, whom he married in 1881. He moved to Oak Park in 1885, upon accepting a position in the Chicago law office of Anna's cousin, John P. Wilson.

In his *Autobiography,* Wright tells a charming story about how he gained the commission for the Nathan Moore House. Although Wright was aware that Moore, a neighbor since 1889, was planning to build a new house just a short block from his own, he writes that he could not lower himself to actually solicit the commission, even though "[t]hree children were now running around the streets without proper shoes."

In Wright's telling, Nathan and Anna Moore sought him out in his Schiller Building office, armed with photographs of the kind of English Tudor house they wanted. Why they visited Wright in his downtown Chicago office instead of simply walking up the street may be due to the fact that they were some fifteen years older and probably did not know Wright socially. Moore told Wright, "Now we want you to build our house . . . but—I don't want you to give us anything like that house you did for Winslow. I don't want to go down backstreets to my morning train to avoid being laughed at."

Writing more than thirty-five years after the event, Wright claimed he took the commission for the money: "at any rate it was the one time in the course of a long career that I gave in to the fact that I had a family and they had a right to live—and their living was up to me." While he claimed to be embarrassed when people admired the home he built, he did declare that it "was the first time . . . an English half-timbered house saw a porch."

It certainly did have a porch and was as handsome a Tudor house as Wright, or anyone else, could have created. The gables—two smaller ones on the front and one at the rear, with larger end gables—had fairly complicated half-timbering. The house was sited at the north (Superior Street) end of the lot. Visitors often mistake the door on this side of the house for the front door when approaching for the first time.

This confusion became even more marked when Wright rebuilt the house in 1923, after it was badly damaged by a fire on Christmas Day 1922. In addition to lowering the roofline from the second to the first floor lintel line, he replaced the formerly narrow chimneys with extraordinarily broad ones, with terra-cotta moldings at their ends, which would not have seemed out of place in his famous Imperial Hotel in Tokyo (1915, demolished 1968). Wright's famous porch, while not changed in form, now has terra-cotta screens at each end that can only be described as Meso-american. They resemble the concrete "textile blocks" that he designed for various Southern California clients from 1917 to 1923, particularly those for the Ennis and Freeman Houses (both 1923).

As for the bay windows with Gothic tracery on the east and north sides of the house, the reminiscences of a former neighbor may shed some light. Lucy Thomas Doering was born in 1906 in Wright's Frank Thomas House, located two short blocks south of the Moore House. She recalls Wright telling her mother during a visit that the Moores' daughter Marjorie, who was an architect, had participated in the 1923 rebuilding and that the result was "Marjorie's house."[1] Since Wright clearly signed the plans, and his onetime employee Charles White (1876–1936) was hired to supervise construction, Marjorie Moore's participation is purely speculative but nonetheless intriguing.

■

Above right: Two dormer windows and a Gothic bay were added in 1923 to dress up the formerly restrained north façade that faces the street.

Below right: The Moore House as it appeared prior to the 1922 fire. The Tudor half-timbering in the gables is more pronounced and more typical of the style than the remodeled version, as are the diamond-paned bay windows above the porch. Photograph by Philander W. Barclay, 1896. Courtesy the Historical Society of Oak Park and River Forest.

[1] Lucy Thomas Doering, videotaped interview by Karen Brammer and Kevin Murphy, November 26, 1996, courtesy Karen Brammer.

39

NATHAN G. MOORE HOUSE

The steeply pitched, dormered roof of the CHAUNCEY WILLIAMS HOUSE was more common to the work of Wright's British contemporaries than to his own canon. Looking at the façade, we would expect the octagon at the left to be part of the living room; actually it is the library, the living room being placed at the back of the house. Instead of the easy transition from the living to dining rooms that is typical in most Wright homes, one must travel back through the reception area to reach the living room. Nor is the library accessible, except from the living room.

CHAUNCEY WILLIAMS HOUSE

5

1895

The Chauncey Williams House—with its steeply pitched roof, dormer windows, boulder-flanked entry and base, and quatrefoil front window—is unique in Wright's work. While it shares materials (Roman brick and plaster) with the earlier Winslow and the contemporary Nathan Moore Houses, it has no discernible stylistic antecedents. If the Winslow develops Sullivanesque ideas and the Moore is unabashedly Tudor, what are we to make of the Williams?

Chauncey Williams had studied in England for a year before attending the University of Wisconsin at Madison, so we might speculate that he and his new friends—the Wrights, Wallers, and Winslows—had perhaps discussed the work of such British architects as Philip Webb, Richard Norman Shaw, and C. F. A. Voysey. Influenced by William Morris and the Arts and Crafts movement, this group of architects put a premium on the use of local materials and simple forms.

This would certainly go a long way in explaining the use of boulders from the bed of the nearby Des Plaines River, apparently—and romantically—carried to the building site by the young friends. The steeply pitched, dormered roof was another feature not uncommon in the work of the British architects, some of whom were Wright's contemporaries. He almost certainly would have seen their work in British architectural journals.

Williams was born in Milwaukee in 1872, but his family later moved to Madison, where his father was a partner in a farm machinery company. Although the son apparently did not know Frank Lloyd Wright during this period, his family did know Wright's mother's family, the Lloyd Joneses, and this led Chauncey Williams, newly married and with an inheritance of one hundred thousand dollars, to look up Wright when he moved to Chicago.

He thus entered the Wright-Waller-Winslow circle, buying his building lot from Edward Waller. The land was just a block east of the Winslow House and part of the original Waller estate. His partnership with Wright and Winslow in the Auvergne Press has already been noted (see page 31).

Williams managed the Turner Brass Works in Chicago before establishing the publishing company of Way & Williams in 1895. One of the firm's authors, essayist William Allen White, mentions the house in his autobiography as a place where fireside chats were held in a "big living room with a wide, hospitable hearth at one end."

The front entrance
area is flanked by
boulders from the
nearby Des Plaines
River. The quatrefoil
window is unique in
Wright's work.

Wright redesigned the dormers after 1900. This original dormer survives on the north façade. The later dormers more clearly echo the roof design, and their overhanging eaves provide better protection for the windows.

A view of the octagonal library, with its Roman-brick fireplace and bookcases. Additional built-in cabinets line the arched hallway leading to the living room, whose beamed ceiling resembles those used in the Harrison P. Young and Nathan Moore Houses of the same period.

HARRISON P. YOUNG HOUSE

6

1895

The 1895 Harrison P. Young House is one of several that Wright remodeled during the Oak Park years. In two later cases—the 1900 Hills and 1906 Beachy Houses—Wright's redesign completely obscured the original house, which provided little more than structural elements. In two other existing houses—the 1896 Charles E. Roberts and 1909 William Copeland—Wright's remodeling was primarily interior.

Wright's raw material in this case was a simple frame house built sometime before 1873 by William Coman, who had purchased the property from Oak Park's founder, Joseph Kettlestrings. In 1892, the modest house was sold to Harrison P. Young and his wife, Lizzie. Young was a purchasing agent for the Fraser & Chalmers Company, a predecessor to the tractor manufacturer Allis-Chalmers. With two growing daughters, the Youngs apparently felt the need to enlarge their small house; they hired Wright, who lived barely a block away, to carry out the project.

The existing house was moved back sixteen feet and an addition with a distinctive front porch was added to fill this space. The cruciform plan with prominent crossed gables is reminiscent of Wright's own home and of the 1893 Clark House in LaGrange, Illinois. Wright's persistent interest in the gable form is evidenced by its use in the early Prairie houses he designed in 1900 in Kankakee, Illinois, for the Bradley and Hickox families. The 1906 Beachy House in Oak Park has no fewer than seven gables.

While Wright's own home has an open porch, or veranda, the Young House has a covered wraparound porch with semicircular ends. The south end, originally open, was enclosed by a later owner. Also added later was the decorative half-timbering on the gable, which does not appear on Wright's original plans. Whether he added them during construction—a common practice for him—cannot be known with certainty, since no photograph of the house without them has been found.

Absent the half-timbering, exterior decoration is restrained. Geometric pilasters flank the band of three diamond-paned casement windows above the porch. All three gables have arched Gothic windows at the attic level.

■

The HARRISON P. YOUNG HOUSE has a carriage-level entry to its porch, protected by a bracket-supported porte cochere.

A view from the reception area to the living room, showing a Roman-brick fireplace and beamed ceilings not unlike the Chauncey Williams House of the same year. The door to the right of the fireplace leads to the southern end of the porch, which was enclosed by a later owner.

47

Wright rarely used clapboard siding, but it is effectively handled in the HARRY C. GOODRICH HOUSE, with a stringcourse running below the upstairs windows to provide a color transition. Although the basement extends above grade, the lower clapboards extend to the ground to obscure the foundation. The dormers (one in the front and two at the rear), a later addition, were not designed by Wright, but they fit the character of the house.

HARRY C. GOODRICH HOUSE

1896

GEORGE W. SMITH HOUSE

1896

7

Harry Clinton Goodrich typified the inventors of the nineteenth century who made their fortunes looking for ways to lighten the domestic load. His patents totaled more than a hundred, the most successful of which was a tuck marker for sewing machines. In an age when home sewing was almost universal, this 1891 patent earned him over four hundred thousand dollars. Another invention, a simple felt border for school slates, earned royalties of more than forty-five thousand dollars. In an era when five thousand dollars a year was a substantial income, Goodrich was earning princely sums.

Apparently, however, Goodrich—like his architect—always spent more than he earned. A local newspaper story in 1906 describes a new ladies' hair dryer that he hoped, at the age of seventy-five, would restore his fortunes. While his inventions have not survived, the house Wright designed for him in 1896 has perpetuated his name. Originally one of a series of five speculative unbuilt designs for Wright's friend and supporter Charles Roberts, it was recycled and refined for Goodrich.

Nearly square in plan, with a prominent central bay and porch extension, the house still looks back to the Queen Anne style, while its angularity looks forward to Wright's increasing interest in linear and geometric forms. The steep roof flares out at the bottom to form very wide overhanging eaves, typical of the later Prairie houses. The porch—originally open—is similar to the form used on the two Furbeck Houses of 1897.

The George W. Smith House of the same year has a different roof form and varies in other details, but it too is based on the Roberts designs. Smith was a buyer for Marshall Field & Company and, like so many of Wright's clients, a Unitarian.

■

Above: This view of the Goodrich House living room shows it as it appeared after Frank Lloyd Wright made changes in 1908 for new owners. A wall that had separated the sitting room from the library was removed, apparently to accommodate a grand piano. The ceiling beams were added to provide structure lost when the wall was removed. Wright also added the benches flanking the fireplace.

Right: A view of the reception area in the Goodrich House, showing the main staircase. The stairway, with its built-in seat and turned spindles, is similar in form to that in Wright's own home. The light fixture, which is original, was powered by both gas and electricity.

The GEORGE W. SMITH HOUSE originally had a wood-shingle roof and open front porch.

The ROLLIN FURBECK HOUSE represents a way station on Wright's journey to his Prairie houses of 1900 and later. While it retains some traditional elements—like the loggias with their decorative columns and dentil molding under the eaves—the low, hipped roof and wide, overhanging eaves look forward to the use of these elements in most of the mature Prairie houses.

GEORGE AND ROLLIN FURBECK HOUSES

8

1897

The Furbeck Houses—designed for brothers George and Rollin Furbeck—are among a group that mark Wright's initial movement away from more traditional styles to the forms that would lead to his Prairie houses at the turn of the century.

It has long been believed that the houses were wedding gifts to the brothers from their father, Warren, who moved to Chicago in 1861 and settled in Oak Park in 1866; later family recollections, however, suggest that the brothers repaid their father over time. Warren married Sophia Whaples in 1871 (her family was the second to settle in Oak Park) and began his business career as a banker with the First National Bank in Chicago. In 1882, he left the bank to join Charles T. Yerkes, then engaged in creating a monopoly in Chicago's burgeoning street railway and rapid transit systems. By 1892, Furbeck was vice president of the North Chicago Street Railway Company, Yerkes' holding company. He left Yerkes before a series of scandals forced Yerkes to sell out in 1900 and return to New York, where he became involved in financing the London subway system. In 1899, Furbeck started his own stock and bond brokerage, W. F. Furbeck & Company, after working briefly for A. L. Dewar.

At the time his house was commissioned in 1897, son Rollin was also employed at Dewar. His brother George was listed in local directories variously as an electrician, coal merchant, and manufacturer's representative. Both brothers married in 1897 and moved their brides into two very different Wright houses.

George Furbeck got a highly geometric composition, a long rectangle with octagonal turrets in front, flanking a covered porch and entrance. Adding to the geometry, the turrets are capped with circular roofs. The south turret encompasses a first-floor library and part of the master bedroom on the second floor. The north turret houses the stairway, its windows bringing light into this space.

The house designed for Rollin points more clearly to Wright's future development. While the prominent three-story central tower is a decidedly vertical element, reminiscent of the 1897 Heller House in Chicago, Wright has also emphasized the horizontal with the roof forms and the use of limestone trim to define the various levels. Both the living and dining rooms have large picture windows, perhaps their first residential use, but one that Wright himself would rarely repeat.

Two changes, possibly by Wright, were made to the Rollin Furbeck House in 1907: the south porte cochere was enclosed to make a sun porch, and the dining room was enlarged to include the original back porch. Recent restorations have greatly improved the condition of the house; additions and modernizations, all at the rear, have not unduly affected its integrity.

■

The GEORGE FURBECK HOUSE as built, showing the original open porch (later enclosed). Wright included a balcony between the turrets with access from the master bedroom. A porte cochere, since removed, provided access for carriages along the north driveway. Photograph by Philander W. Barclay, 1903. Courtesy the Historical Society of Oak Park and River Forest.

This detail shows the octagonal bay and turret of the George Furbeck House. Although simple common brick is used, the pink mortar and overlapping corners provide heightened visual interest.

Above: The George Furbeck living room is a full octagon, as is the library, visible through the door at the left. The window seat is a more modern replacement of the original. The carpet was designed by the home owners to highlight the room's shape.

Right: A service hall in the George Furbeck House runs behind the living room fireplace (whose Roman brick is visible to the right), originally providing the servants with access to the front door. Niches with spindled screens on both sides of the fireplace permit north light to enter from the hallway windows.

The ends of the George Furbeck dining room alcove reinforce the octagonal motif. The table and overhead light fixture were commissioned by the home's residents of thirty-five years. Screenlike art-glass windows complement the Japanese ceramics.

Above: The Rollin Furbeck fireplace, with its precast concrete panels, is unique among Wright's inglenooks.

Right: The second-floor columns, seen here through the windows of the Rollin Furbeck master bedroom, are purely decorative. Their stylized leaf capitals reflect the ideas of Wright's mentor, Louis Sullivan. Such decorative effects would become increasingly rare in Wright's work and when used—as in the columns of Unity Temple—would be far more abstract.

This intimate space in the Rollin Furbeck House is on the landing above the entrance hall (the front door is visible at right).
Wright had not yet abandoned double-hung windows, although he used the more typical casement windows in the bay,
which overlooks the front porch.

Ah! I have found a nice quiet and unmolested (hitherto) page
to leave a hidden note of love and appreciation for my dear
friend. I will speak for the whole of the Tutaj clan (which at the
time of printing consists of me, Emily and goldendoodle) in saying
we so greatly love and cherish you, Alison, Helena and Charlotte,
and refuse to think of you as anything less than family.
We look forward to more good times. Mike

The HILLS-DeCARO HOUSE reflects the influence of Japanese art and architecture on Wright's work. The roof forms, in particular, are very similar to those on the Ho-o-den buildings at the Japanese exhibit at Chicago's Columbian Exposition of 1893.

HILLS-DeCARO HOUSE

1900, 1906

9

Between 1895, when Wright designed Nathan Moore's Tudor mansion, and 1900, when Moore asked him to move and remodel an existing house on his property, the once-wary client must have had a change of heart about Wright's unconventional architecture. The remodeled house, now known as the Hills-DeCaro House, was decidedly more in keeping with Wright's developing style than the Tudor design Moore had previously demanded for himself (see page 37 for Wright's version of the story).

Within the Hills-DeCaro House, but entirely hidden, is the structure of the original Stick-style Gray House, which Moore bought in March 1900 with the intent of remodeling and giving to his daughter Mary when she married. Construction did not begin until 1906, to a plan substantially revised from Wright's design of 1900; Mary did not marry until 1908; and she and her husband, Edward Rowland Hills, did not occupy the house until 1911.

Hills was born in Cincinnati in 1874, the son of a Presbyterian minister. He was a graduate of Wooster College and the Cincinnati Law School. Perhaps because his mother, Louise Freer, was a member of a prominent Chicago family,

he moved to Chicago and was admitted to the Illinois bar in 1902. He met Mary Moore at Oak Park's First Presbyterian Church in 1906. Their connection to the church was strong: later, three of the Hillses' five sons would become Presbyterian ministers, and the church would name a chapel in Mary's honor.

Neither Edward nor Mary Hills seemed taken with Wright's architecture. According to their son John's reminiscences in a letter, "My parents idea on the Wright houses was that some of them were pleasing, many of them were queer, and all of them were inconvenient and needed alteration." John also wrote that his mother found Wright's work "too stern and austere."[1]

Before they finally moved in, the Hills hired local architect Henry Fiddelke, who lived just around the corner on Superior Street, to carry out a series of alterations. He divided the master bedroom into two rooms and changed its four-window bay into a pair of two-window bays, added another bedroom, remodeled the kitchen, enclosed the rear porch, and excavated under the porch to create a children's playroom. Now presumably more content with the house, Mary stayed after Edward's death until 1965.

The house eventually suffered the same fate as its neighbor, the Moore House. On January 3, 1976, a fire largely destroyed the structure above the first floor. The built-in china cabinet in the dining room was spared. On its top was a set of Wright's original plans that miraculously remained undamaged. The DeCaros, who then owned the house, spent the next two years returning it to a condition much closer to Wright's intentions than the much-changed house that had burned. The extensive restoration required 136 new windows to be manufactured and more than two miles of trim to be custom-milled and installed.

With its deeply pitched roof with flared eaves (which it shares with the earlier George W. Smith House), smooth stucco surfaces, and restrained window designs, the Hills-DeCaro House is said to be one of Wright's most Japanese-influenced designs. While he would not actually travel to Japan until 1905, by 1900 he was already a collector of Japanese woodblock prints and other objects.

Wright would later write that he was influenced not so much by Japanese architecture as by an aesthetic that pared things down to their essential forms. At the time he designed the Hills-DeCaro House, Wright was using the same principles to create an entirely new American architecture. While this house might still be considered transitional, it was followed almost immediately by the Bradley and Hickox Houses (both 1900) in Kankakee, Illinois, considered the first of the Prairie houses, and in 1901 by the first of the truly great Prairie houses, the Ward Willits House in Highland Park, Illinois.

■

---

[1] John M. Hills to Carol Kelm, January 17, 1985, Frank Lloyd Wright Preservation Trust Research Center.

The living room fireplace is made of Wright's favorite Roman brick. The mosaic mural is a recent addition. The light fixture to the right is a copy of a design Wright used in the living and dining rooms of the famous Robie House (1908–1910) in Chicago, among others.

The dining room features the china cabinet that survived the 1976 fire. The table and chairs are not original but are based on Wright's designs of the period. The ceiling fixture, said to be from Mexico and clearly not a Wright design, was installed by the Hills. When he later visited the house, Wright asked, "What are those tonsils hanging down from the ceiling?"[2]

[2] Mr. and Mrs. Nathan Grier Hills, recorded interview by Sandra Bottoms and Jane Kenamore, November 13, 1988, Frank Lloyd Wright Preservation Trust Research Center.

The bay window on the upstairs landing provides a view of the Moore House to the north. The whimsical light fixture is based on a design Wright used in the playroom of his Oak Park home.

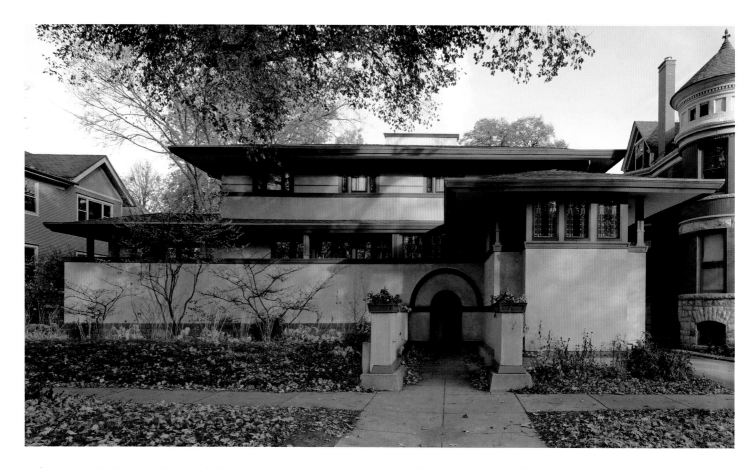

In the FRANK W. THOMAS HOUSE, the low, hipped roof, long bands of second-floor windows, third-floor trim, and broad chimney all emphasize the horizontal. The third-floor windows are unique, being Wright's take on the famous Chicago window, used in so many early Chicago commercial buildings, wherein a large fixed window is flanked by movable sashes. Behind the windows were four bedrooms, although a later addition altered the layout.

FRANK W. THOMAS HOUSE

1901

10

The Frank W. Thomas House was commissioned by James C. Rogers for his daughter Susan and her new husband, Frank Thomas. Rogers, who had built a substantial house in Oak Park in 1881, was a longtime member of the Chicago Board of Trade. Frank Thomas was also a member of the Board of Trade and the Chicago Stock Exchange, and at the time of the marriage in 1900 was employed by the stockbrokers A. O. Slaughter & Company, from which he eventually retired as senior partner.

Whether or not it was a wedding present, as has been generally accepted, is open to question, since Lucy Thomas Doering, daughter of Susan and Frank Thomas, noted that her parents made regular payments to Rogers for many years. She also said that because Wright had the reputation of being "a little slippery," her grandfather kept a tight rein on the budget.[1]

Wright's friend Edward C. Waller, for whose River Forest estate Wright was then designing stables, may have had a role in guiding Rogers to his architect. The two businessmen were close; indeed, the Wallers hosted a prewedding dinner for Susan and Frank Thomas. Susan, who had studied the violin in Germany and writing at the Lewis Institute in Chicago,

and who had a lifetime love of poetry and the arts, may also have played a role in choosing Wright.

The commission gave Wright his first opportunity to build one of his new Prairie houses in Oak Park. Beginning in the late 1890s, he had been moving toward the creation of a new Midwestern architecture, one that would not be beholden to Old World forms but that would embrace both American values and the American prairie landscape. The Thomas House has been compared to Wright's design for "A Home in a Prairie Town," published in the *Ladies' Home Journal* of February 1901. Designed for an ideal prairie landscape, the *Journal* house is very wide, including a covered veranda on one end, a porte cochere on the other, and a privacy wall for the gardens behind.

For the Frank W. Thomas House, Wright had a building lot only one hundred feet wide, although it was a generous two hundred feet deep. It had been the location of the first Grace Episcopal Church, torn down when Rogers and his fellow church members decided to build the current church nearby on Lake Street. Hemmed in by houses that still exist today, Wright chose a three-story, L-shaped plan and placed the house at the front of the lot, providing views up Forest

Avenue and across to Austin Gardens, a park that was donated to Oak Park by pioneer citizen Henry Austin.

A narrow driveway on the south side of the house was added after the house was sold in 1961. According to Lucy Thomas Doering, the family car was kept in a commercial parking garage and was picked up as needed.

Save for an arch that provides entry, the first level of the Thomas House is hidden behind a wall; it originally included only service areas and servants' quarters, but the family later converted some of the space into a playroom. A door behind the arch is actually the basement door. In typical Wright fashion, a "path of discovery" leads to the main entrance: one must go upstairs to the left, then right, to finally discover that what had appeared to be one of a row of art-glass windows from the sidewalk is actually a door.

Despite the scandal that followed Wright's love affair with Mamah Cheney and subsequent desertion of his wife and family in 1909, many of his clients remained loyal to him. Lucy Thomas Doering recalled that whereas Frank Thomas took a dim view of Wright's morals, Mary Thomas continued to welcome his occasional visits (always when her husband was at the office). After Wright moved to Wisconsin, he maintained an office in Chicago for many years and would stop by when he was in Oak Park. On one such visit, Wright had spent about forty-five minutes chatting with Mary, when he suddenly exclaimed that he had to leave because he had left "Carl" waiting. Wright had been showing his friend Carl Sandburg some of his local work and left him in Austin Gardens across the street while he stopped in to say hello to his former client. Lucy Doering also confirmed that Wright designed a large living room table and at least two chairs for the house. She said her parents found them unsuitable and got rid of them.

Several changes have been made to the house over the years. In 1922, a three-story addition was added to the rear, creating a new library on the main floor and another bedroom on the third floor. Although the architects of record are Tallmadge & Watson, Lucy Thomas Doering claimed that family friend Charles E. White, who worked for Wright from 1903 to 1905, executed the actual design. In any event, the design was entirely sympathetic to Wright's own.

∎

1 Lucy Thomas Doering, videotaped interview by Karen Brammer and Kevin Murphy, November 26, 1996, courtesy Karen Brammer.

Right: A magical entry surrounds the visitor with sparkling glass. The facing door is the open front door. The entry to the interior of the house is at the left. The photograph was taken through another door that leads to the veranda.

Left: A "path of discovery" leads to the front entrance. This view shows the arched entryway, with a pier and lantern on the level above. The door visible through the arch is the basement door. The main entry door is to the right of the lantern. From the sidewalk, it appears identical to the windows on the main level.

Below: The beaded decoration on the entry pier is echoed in the ornamentation on the dining room's built-in china cabinet. The glass design is based on Native American arrow forms.

A view of the dining room, looking northwest. Although not original, the table is based on Wright designs.

Lucy Thomas Doering, who grew up in the house, remembers sitting on the built-in couch in the alcove,

watching for her father to come home from the office.

Above: The exterior of the Davenport House. It has been restored, but the former open front veranda has not been rebuilt.

Right: The Davenport House is based on this 1901 rendering for the *Ladies' Home Journal.* Conceived for a wider lot than that of the Davenport House, the design allows for a porte cochere on the right and a separate wing to the left for the dining room.

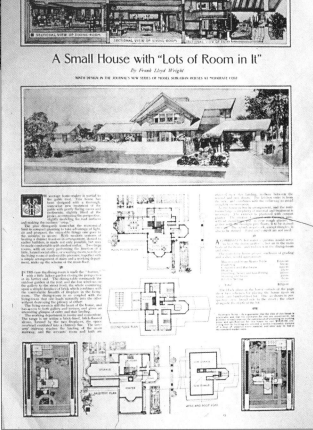

E. ARTHUR DAVENPORT HOUSE

11

1901

Wright's national reputation was enhanced by a series of designs he did in the early 1900s for the *Ladies' Home Journal.* The house he designed in 1901 for E. Arthur Davenport and his wife, Susan, was largely based on the "Small House with Lots of Room in It" that appeared in the July 1901 issue. With its gabled roof forms, it also resembled the 1900 Bradley and Hickox Houses, considered the first of Wright's Prairie houses.

Davenport was a longtime passenger agent for the Pullman Company and active in River Forest affairs. He variously served as a village trustee, president of the library board, and township supervisor. He remained in the house until his retirement in 1936, when he moved to California.

Because Davenport's lot was relatively narrow, Wright adapted the *Journal* plan by removing the porte cochere and placing the dining room partially behind the living room rather than in a separate wing. In both designs, the living room faces the street in a compact cruciform plan. It was served by the same open veranda that he provided for the *Journal* house, but to keep the cost down, the exterior of the house was sided with wood boards and battens instead of the stucco specified in the *Journal.*

Like the Fricke and Thomas Houses, the Davenport was built during Wright's brief partnership with Webster Tomlinson (1870–1942), who apparently was brought into the firm to handle administrative matters—never Wright's strongest suit. His detailed statement of construction costs survives, revealing a total cost of less than four thousand dollars, including a three-hundred-dollar architect's fee. It also lists Giannini and Hilgart as suppliers of the handsome, screenlike art-glass windows. Orlando Giannini collaborated with Wright on several commissions, including murals for Wright's own home.

The front of the house was changed in the early 1930s. A veranda and bay window were removed, either because the veranda was in bad condition or to provide more direct light for the living room. The art-glass windows from the bay were reused in the new front elevation.

Above: At the WILLIAM G. FRICKE HOUSE, the restoration of an original garden wall, extending from the house to the garage, forms a continuous sill line that emphasizes the step-down nature of the north façade.

Right: Wright's rendering for the Wasmuth Portfolio shows the pavilion that extended into the south gardens. Its loss makes the Fricke House seem much more vertical than Wright intended. Plate XIX from the series *Ausgeführte Bauten* (June 1910). Collection of the Frank Lloyd Wright Preservation Trust, 1995.17.31.

WILLIAM G. FRICKE HOUSE

The William G. Fricke House was built on two fifty-foot lots at the corner of Fair Oaks Avenue and Iowa Street. The main structure was placed on the north edge of the property, with a connected pavilion extending to the south to provide both physical and visual access to the gardens to the south and east. The pavilion, clearly an important part of Wright's composition, was torn down when a later owner sold the south lot in the 1920s. Without it, Wright's provision of a generous southern exposure was lost, although the lot remained vacant until 1948. The main structure, however, remains largely intact.

Wright designed the house in 1901, during the brief period he was in partnership with Webster Tomlinson. By the time the drawings were published as part of the Wasmuth Portfolio in 1910, it was called the Emma Martin House after the second owner, for whom Wright designed a garage in 1907. But the original clients were William G. Fricke and his wife, Delia.

Born in Germany in 1868, Fricke moved with his family to the United States when he was seven. Very little is known about his early life, but when he was sixteen he was listed in Chicago directories as a bookkeeper. When he married Delia —a native Oak Parker and member of a prominent local family—and moved to Oak Park in 1893, he was working for the Weber Company, a school-supply business. By the time he commissioned his house in 1901, he was a partner in the firm, which was then called the Weber-Costello-Fricke Company.

Although previous accounts have stated that Emma Martin purchased the house in 1907 from Fricke's estate, census and divorce records suggest that Fricke sold the house because of financial difficulties. According to divorce records, William Fricke left for work on August 10, 1909, and never returned. He did not contact his wife again, but was reported to be working for a school-supply company in Dallas the following year. The 1930 census found him living in a San Francisco rooming house.

While the roof forms "step down" on the north and south elevations much as they do in the later Martin House, the Fricke appears more vertical, due not only to its height but also to the art-glass windows and mullions that rise through two stories, leading the eye up to the third floor. The columned loggias provide small balconies leading from what was originally the billiards room. The thin profile of the eaves and defining trim provide a horizontal counter-point to the verticality of the tower.

■

The reception (now music) room features a prow-shaped bay, a favorite motif used by Wright in many buildings, most notably the famous Robie House of 1908–1910.

The east end of the dining room was originally used as a breakfast area and would have had a separate, smaller table for that purpose. The banded trim emphasizes the horizontal while visually lowering the ceiling.

A view from the living room toward the entrance hall and stairs to the second floor. The fireplace brick (right) is Norman, rather than the Roman brick that Wright more commonly used. The hall serves as the main circulation space, providing access to all the first-floor rooms. Every alternate stairway spindle is rotated forty-five degrees, repeating the prow shape of the dining room screens and the music room bay window.

ARTHUR B. HEURTLEY HOUSE

13

1902

In *Frank Lloyd Wright to 1910: The First Golden Age,* Grant Manson groups the Heurtley House with the Charnley and Winslow Houses, describing them as the "great triumvirate." While the last two rank high in the Wright canon, they still owe something to the influence of Louis Sullivan. The Heurtley, however, is clearly in the architect's emerging and distinctive Prairie style.

While it shares a decided horizontality with the Frank Thomas House of the year before, it is quite different in effect. Except for several small stucco panels, the Heurtley House is built of brick and concrete. A low, hipped roof covers the entire monolithic structure. It is admired as much for its uniqueness in Wright's oeuvre as for the refinement and elegance of its details.

In its solidity, the Heurtley House may pay homage to the work of Henry Hobson Richardson, who was America's most admired architect when he died in 1886—the year Wright began his own career. When Wright arrived in Chicago in 1887, Richardson's Glessner House and Marshall Field Warehouse Store had just been completed. When Wright joined Adler & Sullivan later that year, he would have been fully aware of Louis Sullivan's veneration of

Richardson's Romanesque-revival designs, reflected in Sullivan's own designs for the Auditorium Building and Walker Brothers' Warehouse, both completed in 1889.

The building permit specified frame-and-stucco construction like the Thomas House. Although no documentation exists for the change in materials, it may be that Heurtley preferred the more solid and substantial appearance of masonry construction. The house is firmly anchored to the ground with a concrete water table, used even for the low prow-shaped wall that protects the entrance. Two shades of brown brick are set in alternating courses. The mortar used in the vertical joints between the bricks is the same color as the brick, permitting the eye to scan the surface horizontally without interruption. The house has no downspouts, which would have added a discordant vertical element. The rainwater simply pours from the gutters to ground drains. Long bands of art-glass windows heighten the horizontal effect, as does the low wall that extends the composition south to the lot line. The chimney, very low and wide, uses the same brick as the house.

Like so many of Wright's clients, Arthur Heurtley was a businessman with a strong interest in the arts. When the

The ARTHUR B. HEURTLEY HOUSE appears to be entirely above grade but actually has a crawl space beneath 80 percent of it. The first floor includes the music/playroom, guest and servant rooms, and utility spaces. The main family spaces occupy the second level. The living and dining rooms face the street, taking up the entire front of the house, except for an open veranda at the south end. Three bedrooms and a bathroom face the backyard.

house was built, he was secretary of the Northern Trust Company in Chicago, then the bank of choice for Chicago's social and business elite. He joined the Northern Trust when it was organized in 1889, remaining until his retirement in 1920, apparently after a series of strokes.

The lot Arthur and his wife, Grace, chose for their home was only half a block south of Wright's own home and studio. While there is no evidence that Wright and Heurtley were personal friends before the house was commissioned, Heurtley must have known about Wright from mutual friends like the Thomases, Moores, and Winslows. They also shared a deep love of music and may well have met at local concerts. Heurtley belonged to several music societies, including the Chicago Orchestral Association, which founded the Chicago Symphony Orchestra. Not surprisingly, the house designed for him included a "perfectly appointed music room" (now the first-floor playroom), according to a 1906 article in the local *Oak Leaves* newspaper.

After they moved in, the Heurtleys added a breakfast porch that extends over the driveway and installed windows in the formerly open veranda. When they sold the house upon Heurtley's retirement in 1920, they moved to Muscatine, Iowa, Grace Heurtley's hometown.

The new owners were Andrew Porter and his wife, Jane Lloyd Wright Porter, Frank Lloyd Wright's sister. The Porters had an existing storage building remodeled into a garage, not by Wright—who was busy with his California projects—but by local architect E. E. Roberts, whose own home and studio were only half a block away. This garage was removed in 1998 and replaced with one more in keeping with the house.

The Porters owned the house until 1946 but did not use it as their primary residence. For economic reasons brought on by the Depression, they converted the lower level into a separate apartment and rented both units while living largely at "Tan-Y-Deri"—the house in Spring Green, Wisconsin, designed for them by Wright in 1907, when Porter was head of the Hillside Home School, founded by Wright's aunts.

After they sold the house, additional changes were made, including removal of the living room inglenook and dining room breakfront. In 1997, the house underwent a major restoration. All surfaces and trim, both exterior and interior, were returned to their original specifications, finishes, and colors. Art glass was restored or replaced. The inglenook and breakfront were re-created, as was a wood screen that had been removed from the top of the stairs.

Today, passersby enjoy a view virtually identical to that of 1902, a view of one of the very finest early Prairie houses, one that Wright himself claimed, in a ninetieth-birthday greeting to Grace Heurtley, as "one of my best, and you really appreciated it."

The second-floor landing, with the dining room visible through the screen. One of Wright's favorite sculptures, the *Winged Victory of Samothrace*, adorns the pier.

The dining room has indirect lighting, hidden by the continuous cove. At the far end, the breakfast area extends into the prow-shaped bay. The tables and chairs are modern interpretations of Wright designs.

The art-glass laylight and vaulted ceiling in the living room replicate the shape of the house's hipped roof. Although the fireplace is constructed of Roman brick instead of the standard brick used for the exterior, its arch echoes the arched front entrance. This use of complementary forms and motifs is a hallmark of Wright's designs. The furnishings are accurate reproductions of Wright's original designs for the house. The trim is birch, coated with a light stain and high-gloss varnish. The rough-surfaced plaster was painted in shades of brown, ochre, green, and blue, with a base coat applied in one color, then a different color applied over it and rubbed to expose the original below. Visitors to the house, accustomed to seeing Wright interiors repainted in muted colors, are often surprised at the richness of Wright's palette during the Prairie period.

A view of the south-
west corner of the
living room, showing
the Wright-designed
reproduction library
table and hanging
lamp. The art-glass
windows at the left
overlook the covered
veranda. Their
abstract forms,
combining horizontal
and vertical elements,
facilitate views to the
outside while also
affording privacy.

Although the design of the WILLIAM E. MARTIN HOUSE, like that of the Fricke, steps down with three distinct roof levels, the relative absence of vertical elements visually lowers the height.

WILLIAM E. MARTIN HOUSE

14

1903

The merits of the William E. Martin House have been to some extent overshadowed by the importance of its client to Wright's immediate future and lasting reputation.

The story begins in September 1902, when William Martin and his brother Darwin—an executive with the Larkin Company of Buffalo, New York, and William's partner in a Chicago stove polish company—visited Wright's studio because William wanted to build a home in Oak Park. As Wright was out of the office, they met with Walter Burley Griffin. What they saw must have impressed them, for William soon returned, met Wright, and sent a now-famous letter to his brother. "Dear Dar," he wrote, "I have been— seen—talked to, admired, one of nature's noblemen . . . Frank Lloyd Wright." He went on to write not only about plans for his own house, but to promote Wright as the best possible choice for Darwin's planned house in Buffalo and even for his employer's office building: "An office such as Wright can build will be talked about all over the country."

While Wright's relationship with the brothers would have its ups and downs, William's initial enthusiasm led not only to his own 1903 Oak Park home but also, between that year and 1908, to the Darwin Martin House and gardener's cottage, the Larkin Building, and three other houses—all in Buffalo. In 1905, Wright designed the EZ Polish Factory in Chicago for the brothers. In 1927, Darwin and his wife had Wright design a summer residence on Lake Erie, in Derby, New York. He was even commissioned to design a family mausoleum, which Darwin called "Blue Sky" due to its impressive size. Although the Martins' straitened financial circumstances during the Depression did not permit its construction, the Forest Home Cemetery in Buffalo finally built it in 2004, with burial spaces sold to the general public.

Born in New York but raised in Nebraska and Iowa, the brothers were self-made men. Darwin, at age twelve, had moved to Buffalo to work at the Larkin Soap Company with his older brother Frank. By the time he was twenty-seven, Darwin had risen through the ranks to become corporate secretary. William stayed on in Iowa for a time, working as a salesman and eventually joining Larkin also, as a salesman. After moving to Chicago in 1882, William became involved in the stove polish business, forming Martin & Barton with his brother-in-law George F. Barton, and ultimately Martin & Martin with Darwin, who apparently served more as financial backer than active partner.

At various times, both brothers experienced delays in getting plans from Wright, caused primarily by the sheer volume of work in his office during this period. In addition to his designs for them, Wright completed more than seventy-five buildings between 1902 and 1906, including the Susan Dana House (1902) in Springfield, Illinois, the Rookery Building lobby remodeling (1905) in downtown Chicago, and Unity Temple (1906) in Oak Park. When Darwin had problems getting drawings from Wright for the Buffalo projects, William acted on his behalf; and when William became flabbergasted over delays with the EZ Polish Factory, Darwin intervened to smooth things over.

For all these frustrations, the Martin brothers remained remarkably loyal to their architect. Both lent him money at various times and supported him in many other ways. William—despite his sympathy with Wright's long-suffering wife Catherine—even agreed to pick up Wright's luggage upon his 1910 return from Europe, where his liaison with Mamah Cheney had scandalized Oak Park and become fodder for the Chicago papers.

Wright's plans for the William E. Martin House are dated February 24, 1903. The building permit is dated August 13 and specifies a two-story house at a cost of ten thousand dollars. Since the plans predate the permit, and presumably were submitted to get the permit, the "two-story" may have simply been a mistake or a reflection of the original plan. Correspondence between William and Darwin suggests that a playroom and maid's room were originally planned for the basement. Martin's wife, Winifred, objected to this arrangement, so the rooms were moved to a new third floor.

William owned two fifty-foot lots and may have wanted the option to sell the south lot later. This might explain why the house was sited to the north and rose to three stories. Had Wright been given the entire one-hundred-foot frontage to work with, the final design might have been quite different. In 1908, William purchased a third adjacent lot and had Walter Burley Griffin design a formal garden, linked to the house by an arbored pergola.

■

A view of the original gardens designed in 1909 by Walter Burley Griffin, who had supervised the gardens for Darwin Martin in Buffalo while employed by Wright. From the series *Ausgeführte Bauten und Entwürfe von Frank Lloyd Wright* (Berlin: Ernst Wasmuth, 1911). Collection of the Frank Lloyd Wright Preservation Trust, 1983.11.03.

In the entrance hall, the art-glass laylight provides both illumination and a sense of direction. The living room, which opens to the left, is visible through the cutout in the dividing wall.

WILLIAM E. MARTIN HOUSE

The current dining room was formerly the breakfast room; the original is now used as a library/family room. The prow-shaped bay, found in many of Wright's Prairie houses, repeats a shape found on the porch. The table and chairs, while a recent design, are similar to Wright's own furniture of the period.

A view of the EDWIN H. CHENEY HOUSE living room, with the library beyond. The space is continuous, with the dining room opposite the library. Original wall sconces complement the window design. The free-standing lamps were commissioned by the current owner to match the sconces. A vaulted ceiling and other surfaces are trimmed in fir. The furnishings are later Wright designs, part of a series he did in the 1950s for Heritage-Henredon. Photograph courtesy Balthazar Korab Ltd.

EDWIN H. CHENEY HOUSE
1903

The scandal and tragedy that grew out of Wright's house design for Edwin H. Cheney and his wife, Mamah, have, at least to some extent, taken the focus away from one of the architect's most interesting Prairie homes.

The Cheneys met at the University of Michigan. Both graduated in 1892, Edwin in electrical engineering and Mamah in liberal arts. In 1893, she earned her master's degree, a rare accomplishment for a woman at that time. She became a teacher, and in her spare time she translated the works of Goethe and Swedish feminist Ellen Key, who was an advocate of "free love," an interest that she and Wright would later share.

Edwin apparently proposed to Mamah on several occasions during the 1890s; in 1899 she finally married him. They were already friends of the Wrights prior to commissioning Frank to design their home in 1903. The couples were known to have attended concerts together, and Mamah and Catherine Wright had even jointly presented a paper on Goethe at Oak Park's Nineteenth Century Women's Club, of which they were both active members.

Edwin largely entrusted Mamah with matters affecting the new home. Although it is not clear when it started, the architect-client relationship had developed into a full-scale affair by 1907. When Wright traveled to Europe in the fall

of 1909 to supervise the publication of a portfolio of his work by Ernst Wasmuth in Berlin, Mamah met him en route in New York. When her presence with Wright was discovered, it caused a scandal that ultimately led Wright to abandon his family and the Cheneys to divorce in 1911. Catherine Wright would not grant her husband a divorce until 1922. Edwin remarried in 1912 and remained in the home until 1927.

Mamah joined Wright in the home he built for her in Spring Green, Wisconsin, which he called Taliesin, Welsh for "shining brow." On August 14, 1914, she and her two children were among seven people murdered by a disgruntled and apparently insane employee, who also set fire to the house.

The front façade of the Cheney House gives it the appearance of a single-story home. The rear is a full two stories, with the ground level originally including utilities, a playroom, and servants' quarters. Earlier plans had shown a garage instead of the playroom, but the Oak Park authorities did not approve of a garage directly below living spaces.

The main level has living and dining areas in the front, and bedrooms served by a hall that runs behind the fireplace wall. As with the later Balch House, the Cheney has a projecting walled terrace facing the street.

The north and east (rear) façades. As is common with Wright houses, art-glass windows provide both beauty and privacy. The windows on the lower level are clear glass, perhaps as an economy. Note the typical absence of discordant vertical downspouts.

Below right: The second-floor plan, with the living room, dining room, and library in front, and the bedrooms at the back, served by a hallway behind the fireplace, is an updated version of the plan for the Heurtley House. It was used with variations for many of the Prairie houses. Plate XXX-b from the series *Ausgeführte Bauten* (June 1910). Collection of the Frank Lloyd Wright Preservation Trust, 1995.17.42.

Above: Although they no longer exist in their original form, ten-foot front and side walls gave the Cheney House the look and feel of a walled compound. The low, hipped roof and wide, sheltering eaves provide an additional sense of privacy and protection. While passersby may find it difficult to gain visual access, occupants are supplied with ample light and air from bands of art-glass casement windows and generous outdoor space. Plate XXX-a from the series *Ausgeführte Bauten* (June 1910). Collection of the Frank Lloyd Wright Preservation Trust, 1995.17.43.

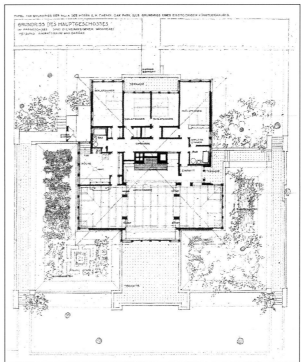

The west façade of the PETER A. BEACHY HOUSE, facing the street, is relatively sedate compared to the south façade (seen here), with its four gables, impressive porch, flanking walls, and typically massive chimney. Wright hid the downspouts within vertical piers. Apparently at Emma Beachy's insistence, there are no art-glass windows in the house; rather, Wright provided casements with wood mullions. On the west façade, he used another version of the Chicago window (see the Frank W. Thomas House), with a large fixed pane flanked by movable sashes.

PETER A. BEACHY HOUSE

1906

16

The practice of naming Wright's houses after the first male occupant sometimes obscures their actual provenance. Although long published as the Peter A. Beachy House, the title to the property was in the name of his wife, Emma, until her death in 1941. Emma's father, Dr. Peter Fahrney, commissioned Wright to do sketches for a home as early as 1901 (the date on the earliest Beachy House drawings at the Frank Lloyd Wright Foundation Archives, Scottsdale, Arizona).

Fahrney was a medical doctor who moved to the Chicago area in 1864 to practice medicine and ultimately to set up a Midwestern branch of the family business—manufacturing patent medicines developed by his father and grandfather, both physicians. His business success and real estate investments, including an eight-hundred-acre farm in Lake County, Illinois, made him a millionaire.

Emma Fahrney was a divorcée with two children, living with her father on Chicago's West Side, when she married Peter Beachy in 1901. She likely met him through her father, for Beachy was then working as an auditor for Dr. Peter Fahrney & Sons Company. After Fahrney's death in March 1905, Beachy seems to have taken over the management of

the estate, since the Oak Park directory lists him variously as "manager of the Dr. Peter Fahrney estate" (1908), "capitalist" (1915), and by 1922, simply as "investments." The investments were lucrative—in 1918 the Beachys had three automobiles (Packard, Hudson, and Baker Electric), a chauffeur, and several other live-in servants.

Wright was likely chosen to design the house thanks to a connection with the Copeland family, who lived a few doors down from the Beachys in a house that Wright later remodeled for them. The Fahrney-Beachy and Copeland families were friends; Emma's son later married a Copeland daughter.

When the property was purchased in 1906 with funds from Peter Fahrney's estate, it had on it a small Gothic cottage that Wright incorporated in his design for the Beachy House. The lot, at 133 by 330 feet, is the largest in Oak Park. Wright sited the house on the north side of the lot, providing the maximum southern exposure and space for extensive gardens.

■

The reception area, with a built-in bench, is open to the second floor. Behind the bench, the stairway rises from right to left. This layout was reversed and the opening closed when the house was converted to two apartments in the 1940s. Later owners restored it to its original form during repairs undertaken after a 1990 fire, which caused considerable damage to the north façade.

A view of the living room, looking south. The hanging light fixtures and wall sconces have the same chevron pattern as the ceiling trim. Wright often chose decorative motifs (here the chevron shape) as unifying elements. The couches were commissioned by a former owner to repeat the angled pattern.

The large dining room includes the original Wright-designed tables and chairs, with the table legs again repeating the chevron shape. Around the main dining table are Wright's typical high-backed chairs, which create a room-within-a-room effect, with smaller chairs used for the subsidiary tables. Light fixtures with pivoting arms, over the near and far tables, have been restored to their original form. French doors lead to a south-facing veranda. The opposite wall has a large fireplace similar to the one in the living room.

UNITY TEMPLE 17
1906

Lightning from the thunderstorm that blew through Chicago and Oak Park early on the morning of June 4, 1905, struck and set fire to numerous church steeples throughout the area, including that of Unity Church in Oak Park. Because of inadequate water pressure, the local firefighters could not get water to the steeple, and the 1872 church burned to the ground.

As it happened, the members of Unity Church had been contemplating a new building that would better suit the needs of a growing congregation, not only for worship but also for expanding social and educational programs. The fire made the decision for them and ultimately provided Frank Lloyd Wright with the opportunity to build what would become one of his most innovative and famous buildings.

A member of the congregation, Wright was well known in Unitarian circles. His mother's brother, Jenkin Lloyd Jones, was a prominent Unitarian minister with a national reputation. Wright's first employer, Joseph Lyman Silsbee, designed All Souls Church on Chicago's South Side for Lloyd Jones. Wright himself, in association with fellow architect and Unitarian Dwight Perkins, had worked on a new mixed-use building for his uncle, to be called the Abraham Lincoln Center. Because uncle and nephew did

not see eye to eye on the project, Perkins ultimately completed the building alone.

Perkins was, in fact, one of four architects the congregation and its pastor, the Reverend Rodney F. Johonnot, considered for designing the new Unity Church. In this competition, Wright's family history in Unitarianism and his local contacts proved decisive. At least four of his Oak Park clients were members of the congregation: Thomas and Walter Gale, George Smith, and Charles Roberts. The Gales' father, Edwin, sold the land for the new church at below-market value. Wright had remodeled Roberts' home and collaborated with him on three unbuilt multihome projects. They were also close friends, and Wright would later credit Roberts—who was on the church building committee—as being the critical factor in his getting the commission.

On September 16, 1905, Wright was announced as the architect. His charge from the congregation was to "construct a church that will be dignified and devotional in aspect, and also suitable to the working needs of a modern church." The building committee hoped that it would be complete and ready for use by September 1906. As it turned out, the first service would not be held until nearly three years later.

Wright's plan for UNITY TEMPLE locates the main entrances behind walls on the building's west and east sides, avoiding busy Lake Street. The columns, with their abstract, conventionalized foliate design, give the building the feel of a Mayan temple.

Wright was given thirty thousand dollars to build, a cost that would exclude only the organ "and other furnishings." The church would ultimately cost some seventy-nine thousand dollars, to the consternation of the congregation.

Wright presented his first schemes in December 1905. With changes, the plans were accepted in March 1906. Ground was broken on May 15. Between that date and final completion in October 1908, the architect made numerous modifications, some due to his choice of reinforced concrete as the primary material instead of the original conception of brick with stone trim, and others when finance-related work stoppages gave him time to rethink interior details.

Concrete was chosen to keep the costs down. Because many of the building's elements, such as piers and columns, are repeated on two or more façades, it was thought that reusing the forms would save money. While this certainly helped, changes to the concrete-aggregate mix, surface treatment, and the addition of reinforcing rods obliterated those savings.

The building lot was on the southeast corner of Lake Street and Kenilworth Avenue, with the longest façade on the Kenilworth side. Wright called the plan "binuclear," by which he meant two complementary structures sharing a common lobby or reception area. It greatly resembled his Oak Park Studio, with its large drafting room, smaller library. and connecting reception room.

The plan locates the main entrances on the west and east sides of the building, insulating them from the noises of Lake Street, then as now a main thoroughfare. Wright further isolated the interior spaces by bringing in outside light mainly from above, either through skylights or clerestory windows placed just under (and protected by) cantilevered overhangs. The columns, with their abstract, conventionalized foliate design, are visible from the interior as well.

With corner piers that act as stair towers, the cubelike structure is similar to Wright's 1903 Larkin Building in Buffalo, New York. In both cases, some observers have mentioned Joseph Maria Olbrich's 1898 Secession Building in Vienna as influencing Wright's use of a solid form and prominent piers. While Wright was known to admire Olbrich, he transformed these ideas into a composition entirely his own.

Unity Temple stands as one of Wright's greatest works, a building that continues to meet the needs of its congregation for worship and community. It is, in the words of the architect himself from his *Autobiography,* a "modern meeting-house and a good time place."

■

Unity Temple is open to the public. For information about tours and other programs, visit the Unity Temple Restoration Foundation's website at www.unitytemple-utrf.org, or call 1-708-383-8873.

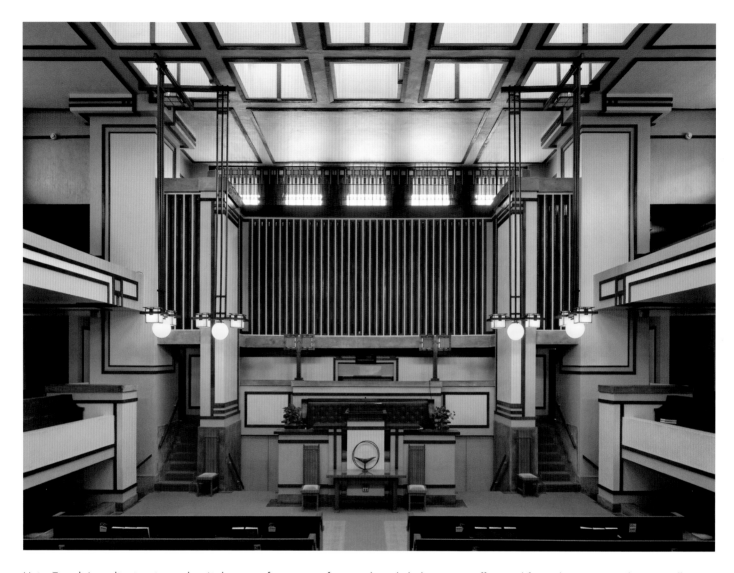

Unity Temple's auditorium is a cube. Light enters from twenty-five art-glass skylights set in coffers and from clerestory windows on all four sides. Wright tinkered with the elaborate wood trim scheme until very late in the construction process. The organ pipes are hidden behind the screen above the pulpit. Exit stairs flank the pulpit. Entry is through the cloisters below the lower balconies. The chairs are reproductions of Wright designs for other buildings. The church can seat more than four hundred people in pews on the main floor and in two balconies on the remaining three sides of the cube.

Above: The exit doors from the auditorium, as seen from the lobby. They have no handles, so are clearly meant for exit only. The lobby has a low ceiling, which Wright often used in transitional spaces to heighten the experience (quite literally) when entering main areas like the auditorium.

Right: Pairs of lancet windows bring natural light into stair towers located in the corner piers. The windows can be seen from the outside only when approached directly.

Unity House serves as the social and educational center for the congregation, hence the fireplace. A large kitchen occupies the space behind it. Initially open, the balconies were later enclosed to provide quieter and more private space for meetings. As in the auditorium, natural light comes mainly from above. The colors here and in the rest of the complex are original.

ISABEL ROBERTS HOUSE 18
1908. REMODELED 1955

On visits to former clients, Frank Lloyd Wright usually took the opportunity to rearrange the furniture to suit his original vision or to give (often unwanted) advice on decorating. But there is only one instance when he returned to remodel an original design: the home he designed in 1908 for his office manager Isabel Roberts, her mother Mary, and sister Charlotte.

As it exists today, the house is an intriguing blend of Wright's Prairie (on the exterior) and Usonian (on the interior) styles. That the new interior does not seem out of step with the exterior is a testament to the simplicity and elegance of Wright's original conception, and to his ability, throughout his long career, to reinvent himself to meet the needs of the times.

Wright used the word *Usonian*—derived from "United States of North America"—to describe his vision for appropriate and affordable housing for middle-class Americans. While he never succeeded in mass-producing the concept, individual houses were built using prefabricated systems that usually included interior wood paneling and space-saving built-in storage, much like that in the Isabel Roberts House.

Wright's decision to remodel the house in 1955 upon the entreaties of the property's then-owners, Warren and Ruth Terry Scott, may well have had something to do with both his fond remembrance of a faithful employee and a nagging recognition that the poor condition of the house may have been, at least to some extent, his fault for cutting corners with the original design.

Although it is called the Isabel Roberts House, Mary Roberts, Isabel's mother, was the owner of record. Isabel had worked for some five years as Wright's office manager before he completed the design. He later said that he did everything possible to keep the cost down, including the use of stucco and wood trim for the exterior. The building permit, issued to Wright's employee William Drummond in September 1908, shows an estimated construction cost of $3,411.

Builders commonly gave a low estimated construction cost on the permit, since the permit fee was based on it. Although it is not clear why, the house was offered for sale in 1910 for nine thousand dollars, which suggests that the actual cost of construction might have been nearly double the amount shown on the permit. However, the house was not sold until May 1923, a year after Mary's death.

The ISABEL ROBERTS HOUSE appears to be a single-story structure from the outside, but it actually consists of three split levels—a revolutionary concept for the time.

By then, Isabel had been living in Orlando, Florida, for seven years, and was a partner with Ida Ryan in an architecture firm. While Isabel may have worked on some glass designs for Wright, she had no architectural training. Thus it seems likely that Ryan, who was the first woman to be granted a master's in architecture at Massachusetts Institute of Technology, was responsible for design and Isabel for administration. Isabel Roberts died in Orlando in December 1955, the year Wright returned to remodel her home.

Two of Wright's colleagues also have connections to the Isabel Roberts House. Prior to Wright's remodeling, his former employee William Drummond—who had built his own home next door to Isabel's on land purchased from Mary Roberts—was commissioned in 1927 to reface the house with brick and replace the wooden sills with cast concrete. He also created a new front entrance and guest closet. Harry Robinson (1883–1959), who worked for Wright both before and after Wright's European trip, lived in the Isabel Roberts House from 1919 to 1923.

In 1955 Wright replaced Drummond's front entrance with a more secluded side entrance. Other changes included converting two small bedrooms into a larger master bedroom, resurfacing the roof with copper, and enclosing and winterizing the side porch. Wright accommodated an English elm in the porch area by letting it grow through the porch roof—reminiscent of the willow that he left growing through the passageway at his Home and Studio.

■

The one-and-a-half-story living room faces west. Ceiling and trim are Philippine mahogany, with broad lapped boards for the vaulted ceiling. The diamond-paned glass remains unchanged. Although Wright designed furniture for the house in 1908, the current furnishings are more in keeping with his 1955 interior.

Above: The Roman-brick fireplace, left unchanged during Wright's 1955 remodeling, faces the living room window. The balcony above was originally part octagon shaped but later simplified to the current three-sided form. Lamps on the balcony level are copies of ones Wright used for his own home, Taliesin, in Wisconsin.

Below: The dining room also features a vaulted ceiling, dominated by a pierced-wood laylight. The elegant built-in cabinets are simpler in form than those of the Prairie period; their sleek lines complement the ceiling. Wright designed the table and chairs for Heritage-Henredon in the 1950s; they fit harmoniously in the redesigned space. The original wood floor on the first level was replaced with flagstones.

The north side of the Roberts House balcony has more built-in cabinetry and generous space to showcase a collection of glass, pottery, and statuary. The windows to the right look out at a forest preserve that stretches from across the street.

LAURA GALE HOUSE

19

1909

The historian and critic Henry Russell Hitchcock, who did much to help restore Wright's reputation in the early 1940s when he published *In the Nature of Materials: The Buildings of Frank Lloyd Wright, 1887–1941,* called the Laura Gale House "a small masterpiece . . . closer to what the Europeans who were most inspired by Wright were to come to in the early twenties."

European architects like Robert van't Hoff and J. J. P. Oud of the Dutch De Stijl movement were greatly influenced by Wright after the 1910 publication of a portfolio of his work in Berlin by Ernst Wasmuth. Among many others, van't Hoff's 1916 A. B. Henny House seems directly influenced by the Gale's distinctive features. Wright himself said, in a catalog for an exhibition of his work at the Guggenheim Museum in 1953, that the Laura Gale House—with its cantilevered balcony and roof forms—was a precursor to the famous Fallingwater in Bear Run, Pennsylvania. The design also resembles that of the 1906 Unity Temple, with which it shares prominent anchoring piers, cubelike forms, and a flat, cantilevered roof.

Wright had known the Gales for many years, designing two houses for Thomas Gale, Laura's husband, in 1892 (see pages 22–24). After Thomas died in March 1907, Laura Gale commissioned Wright to design a new house.

Though modest in size, it was adequate for Laura and her two children. The floor plan is a variation of Wright's economical design "A Fireproof House for $5000," published in *Ladies' Home Journal* in April 1907. The first floor includes a small reception room, living room, dining room, and small kitchen. The second floor has four bedrooms and a servant's room. Two of the bedrooms open onto the second-floor balcony. Even the most modest of Wright's houses had at least one bedroom for a servant; many had two or more. Wright's typical upper-middle-class client would have employed both a cook and a housekeeper.

The house sits on Elizabeth Court, the only curved street in Oak Park (the rest of the village is laid out largely in a continuation of the Chicago grid). Approaching from the west, one does not see the house until the street begins turning to the right. Then the Gale House appears almost magically among the Queen Annes and Victorians that surround it. Wright sited the house near the front of a very narrow lot. The property originally had no garage, but Laura Gale added one later. It did not suit the house and was taken down by a subsequent owner.

Laura Gale lived in the house until her death in 1943. Her daughter Sally lived there until 1961 and was actively involved in the effort to preserve Wright's Oak Park Home and Studio—now a public museum.

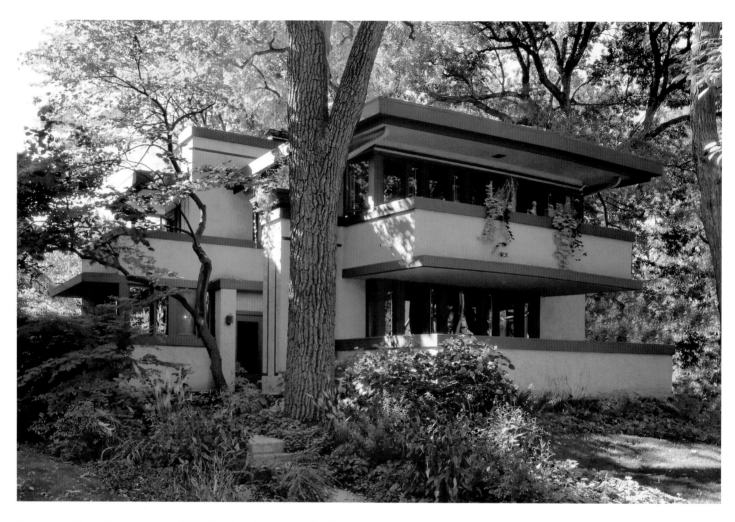

The LAURA GALE HOUSE—one of Wright's best-known smaller houses—presaged his dramatic Fallingwater by thirty-one years.

The sitting area in the west bedroom. The adjacent bedroom shares the balcony. Wright used art glass sparingly, but elegantly, in the Gale House.

The dining room is raised two steps above the living room. Built-in cabinets provide space for books on the living room side and china in the dining room. The windows overlook the back garden.

WILLIAM H. COPELAND HOUSE

1909

20

Dr. William H. Copeland became Frank Lloyd Wright's neighbor in 1898 when he and his wife, Frances, purchased an impressive Italianate home just a few doors south of the architect's Home and Studio. Copeland was born in Ohio in 1860 and trained as a physician at Bellevue Hospital Medical College in New York City. After practicing in Pittsburgh for some years, he and Frances moved to Chicago in 1892, when they had their first daughter, also named Frances. In 1917, daughter Frances married Walter Pratt Beachy, whose parents lived about a block south, in a house Wright had built for them in 1906. Walter became a partner with Wright's son John in the Red Square Company, manufacturers of the famous Lincoln Logs.

By the time Copeland commissioned Wright to remodel his house and garage in 1908, he had retired from his medical practice and was manufacturing patent medicines. Walter Beachy's grandfather, Dr. Peter Fahrney, was in the same business, and they likely would have known each other. With a reputation for their hospitality, the Copelands would also have known other Wright home owners. The Arthur Heurtleys lived next door, and the Moores directly across the street. All would have willingly recommended Wright for Copeland's remodeling job.

The permit for the house is dated August 20, 1909, the month before Wright traveled to Europe to work on the Wasmuth Portfolio, published the following year. Along with the Laura Gale House in Oak Park and the Ingalls House in River Forest (among others), Wright turned over the completion of the Copeland project and the management of his practice to Hermann von Holst (1874–1955), an MIT graduate who was president of the Chicago Architectural Club in 1907, when Wright was a prominent exhibitor in the club's annual show. Wright's assistant John Van Bergen probably handled on-site supervision. The Copelands sold the house in 1929.

■

Frank Lloyd Wright was chosen by the owner to bring the twenty-five-year-old WILLIAM H. COPELAND HOUSE, and its coach house, up to date. The first plans, dated 1908, would have transformed it into a more typical Wright Prairie house. Whether for cost or other reasons, Copeland decided to limit the scope of the work to remodeling the first-floor interior and simplifying the exterior by removing most of the Italianate decorative elements. A two-window dormer serving the attic was replaced with a more linear four-window one, and the roof was changed to provide wider, more sheltering eaves.

The entry hall, with the reception room to the right and living room to the left. Wright used mahogany banding to lower the visual height of the 11½-foot ceilings. Bands of trim also bridge the openings to the rooms.

As is characteristic of Wright's Prairie homes, various design features contribute to a unified environment. The dining room has a three-window bay whose shape is reflected in the ceiling trim. The glass design in the large sideboard is repeated in the door and transom (center) and in the front door as well. Ceiling fixtures match those in the entry hall and reception room.

WILLIAM H. COPELAND HOUSE

The garage was remodeled first (the building permit is dated October 28, 1908) and is much more recognizable as Wright's work than the house remodeling. The pitch of the roof was reduced and the eaves extended. A shop area was added to the south and rows of diamond-paned windows placed under the eaves. The surface was covered with stucco (also specified for the house in Wright's original design, although it kept its original brick surface).

The J. KIBBEN INGALLS HOUSE features a first-floor veranda and second-floor balconies (often used in those days for warm-weather sleeping) in a compact arrangement.

Frank Lloyd Wright visited former clients for a variety of reasons. In some cases, it was simply a matter of visiting an old friend like Susan Thomas of the Frank Thomas House. Other visits may have involved showing a prospective new client the work that the architect had completed for a satisfied home owner. According to the grandchildren of one such satisfied client, Wright visited the J. Kibben Ingalls family in the early 1930s and, having been told how much they had enjoyed the house since moving in, suggested they might pay him an additional fee![1]

While the Ingalls family may have enjoyed their house, Neil Levine in *The Architecture of Frank Lloyd Wright* calls it "labored and vapid in expression." Henry Russell Hitchcock, author of *In the Nature of Materials,* notes, "European imitators . . . often followed this least congenial of Wright's house types of these years." Its form most closely resembles the handsome coach house/garage he did in Chicago for George Blossom in 1907.

When he commissioned Wright in 1909, James Kibben Ingalls was president of the Western Heater Dispatch railroad car company, which he established after having worked for other railroad companies since 1890. In 1925, he founded the North Western Refrigerator Line Company, which leased cars to shippers and railroads. The invention of refrigerator cars made Chicago's immense meatpacking industry possible, and much of Ingalls' business would have depended upon it. When Ingalls died in 1938, his son Allin succeeded his father as president. The company became part of North American Car Company in 1947.

Like many of Wright's clients, Ingalls belonged to both the Oak Park Country Club and the River Forest Tennis Club. He and his wife, Florence, were active in River Forest affairs. Both worked to establish a public library in the village, and he later served on its board, as well as on the boards of the local primary school and high school, serving each as president for long periods.

Their son, Allin, was the only survivor of five children. At least one of the children, Ruth, died of tuberculosis, and family members have cited her illness as the reason why Wright was asked to provide the maximum of light and ventilation in his plans.

In 1917, a detached garage, designed by Wright's former employee William Drummond, was added. In 1926, Drummond added a rear porch that supported a new study and bathroom on the second floor, roughly where the rear balcony had been. A sympathetic 1981 addition expanded the kitchen and added a family room and large terrace to the rear of the house.

■

¹ David Kibben Ingalls and Mary Ingalls Mathewson, telephone interview by Pamela Reynolds, 1999, Frank Lloyd Wright Preservation Trust Research Center.

Wright designed a cruciform plan that provides three exposures for the living and dining rooms. The three second-floor bedrooms also enjoy three exposures to maximize light and ventilation.

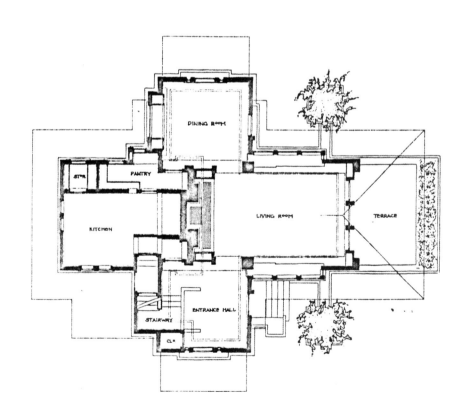

OSCAR B. BALCH HOUSE

Born in Pennsylvania, Oscar B. Balch moved to Oak Park in 1890 to join the pioneer decorating company founded by A. W. and S. E. Pebbles. Eventually, he became a partner with their son Frank in a firm known as Pebbles & Balch. In 1907 Wright remodeled a store for the firm (see page 142 in the chapter on lost and altered structures).

Balch would therefore have known Wright quite well when he commissioned him in 1911 to design his new house. The architect had returned from his European trip in the fall of 1910. Considering the publicity generated by his tryst with Mamah Cheney and subsequent abandonment of his family, he must have welcomed the commission, particularly as it came from an Oak Parker, who would have been fully aware of Wright's private problems.

Since Balch and his wife, Neenie, had four children, Wright provided five bedrooms for the family. In plan, the house resembles the Cheney House. The main rooms of the first floor are in a line, with the central living room extending outward to its walled veranda. The dining room and reception room/library flank the living room. While the bedrooms in the Cheney House lie behind these spaces on the same floor, the Balch bedrooms are on the second floor.

As in so many of the Prairie houses, the entrance is hidden from obvious view, only becoming apparent when you reach the south side of the house. A major, sympathetic addition to the rear provides an enlarged kitchen and two-story family room.

Balch's wife died in 1932, but he stayed in the house until his retirement in 1942. He then moved back to his native Pennsylvania, where he died in 1955.

■

A belvedere-like overlook (just visible above the main roofline at left) is an unusual feature of the OSCAR B. BALCH HOUSE.
The row of five casement windows on the second floor belongs to the master bedroom.

A view of the living room, facing southwest toward the reception area. The fireplace uses Wright's favored Roman brick. A screen above the built-in bookcases hides the stairway to the second floor and a hall that runs behind the fireplace. Similar screening hides the radiator under the art-glass window to the left. The consistency of these features, and the use of wall and ceiling banding to unify the spaces, are hallmarks of Wright's interior designs. Furnishings are modern, but Wright-inspired.

The dining room has the original wooden-framed, art-glass ceiling fixture installed—as was typical of Wright—to offer little leeway in table placement. The reception room/library, at the opposite end of the first floor, has an identical fixture. The art-glass design on the china cabinet doors is a variation of that used on the window above. High-backed chairs are Wright-inspired modern pieces.

Wright provided generous closets at the entrance to the master bedroom. The five casement windows, which face east, have clear panes divided by wood mullions, instead of the art glass of the first floor. Drapes keep out the morning light. In addition to the room's more generous ceiling height, small balconies accessible on both sides further enhance its space and light. In an era without air conditioning, protected balcony spaces were often used for sleeping on warm nights.

Wright's mastery of his Prairie vocabulary produced an elegant home for HARRY S. ADAMS. The low, hipped roof, overhanging eaves, bands of windows, raked mortar in the bricks' horizontal joints—all are hallmarks of Wright's mature Prairie designs. The only obvious change from the house as built is the enclosure of a once-open veranda next to the porte cochere, along with that of a breakfast porch and balcony above it on the rear (north side).

HARRY S. ADAMS HOUSE

23

1913

It is probably safe to say that Harry Stiles Adams was not among Wright's favorite clients. He wanted a fairly elaborate house, and specifically a Wright house, but apparently he was not willing to pay the cost.

Adams was born in 1871 and grew up in Warren, Ohio. He married Florence Vandenburg in 1899 or 1900 and appears in the Oak Park directory for the first time in 1900 as manager of the stationery department at the Schlesinger & Mayer department store (now Carson Pirie Scott) in downtown Chicago. When he built his Wright house, he was the local manager for Eaton, Crane & Pike Company, manufacturers of fine stationery.

The Adamses lived in various locations in Oak Park and River Forest until they moved into their new house in 1914. They would thus have been quite familiar with Wright's local work and with the scandal that surrounded his trip to Europe with his mistress, Mamah Cheney. Nevertheless, they sought him out late in 1911 or early 1912. By April, the architect was writing to his friend Darwin Martin that his new client had "approved early sketches."

The Harry S. Adams House, as it exists today, was at least the third version that Wright designed after the initial sketches. The first design, finished in September 1912, was cross-axial and included a large veranda to the south, with kitchen, traffic areas, and attached garage to the north. The main living areas were on the east-west axis, with each of the three bedrooms having access to a balcony. The cost to build this design far exceeded the thirteen thousand dollars that Adams had budgeted. The building permit for the final version, which eliminated the veranda, attached garage, bedroom balconies, a privacy wall, and other features, was finally issued in November 1913, showing an estimated cost of fifteen thousand dollars.

While Adams apparently had agreed to increase the budget, he did not do so without a fight. Before finally approving Wright's third effort, he had William Gray Purcell (1880–1965) and his partner George Elmslie (1871–1952) take a crack at designing a "Wright" house that would include everything he wanted, but for the original thirteen-thousand-dollar budget. According to Purcell's recollections, written in the 1930s, he and Elmslie did not succeed in meeting Adams' requirements any better than Wright did. Purcell claims that Adams had the temerity to show his firm's sketches to Wright, who predictably was unhappy with both Adams and the "pla-giarizing" architects.

Adams may not have gotten everything he wanted, but he did get a handsome house, the last one Wright would build in Oak Park. It was constructed on a particularly generous lot, originally almost an acre, with 198 feet of frontage on Augusta Street. The house was placed at the east end of the lot, leaving room for extensive gardens, which were mentioned as Florence Adams' particular passion in her obituary in 1927. The west eighty feet were sold off in 1953, although less harm was done by this reduction than was the case with the Fricke and Martin houses.

■

Continuous bands of trim link the sideboard in the dining room with the living room fireplace to unify the design. To integrate the inside with the outside, Wright used the same brick and concrete for the fireplace as for the exterior.

A characteristically sheltered front entrance, with a wooden, woven-grille laylight and art-glass entry door whose panes glisten in iridescent reds, blues, greens, and golds. From the inside, the panes become a more muted green and gold only. Planters, like the one at the left, are ubiquitous in Wright's Prairie buildings; they provide a way to integrate nature in the fabric of the building.

These living room windows face south. The wooden casework of the window seat conceals hot-water radiators. The wall sconces—wood with stencil-like copper bulb enclosures—are a departure from Wright's former art-glass or brass fixtures, and they perhaps signal his movement to a newer design vocabulary as typified by Midway Gardens, which he was working on at the time. Most of the windows on the first floor are plain glass, with the exception of the lancet windows at the far right and those on the opposite wall in the dining room, which face the house next door and were likely used for privacy.

Wright's sure hand with built-in furniture is evident in this handsome sideboard/china cabinet, which eliminates the need for space-consuming freestanding pieces.

24

LOST, ALTERED, AND POSSIBLY WRIGHT

While Oak Park and River Forest have retained most of the structures Wright designed for the two communities, some have been lost or so substantially changed that his hand is no longer apparent.

■

H. W. BASSETT HOUSE REMODELING, OAK PARK, 1894

In 1894, Wright remodeled a house on South Oak Park Avenue to provide living and office space for homeopathic physician Howard W. Bassett. He created a sheltered entrance to the first-floor office and used board-and-batten siding up to the third-floor sill. The porch spindles are the same pattern he used for the playroom balcony in his own home. The building was demolished in the 1920s to make way for commercial development. Photograph courtesy Oak Park Public Library, Oak Park, Illinois.

ROBERTS HOUSE AND STABLE, OAK PARK, 1896

Charles E. Roberts, a long-time friend and supporter of Wright, is credited with getting him the Unity Temple commission. In addition to designing two unbuilt groups of houses for Roberts (the Goodrich and Smith houses are variations of these designs), Wright carried out some remodeling projects in 1896 in Roberts' home, originally designed by Daniel H. Burnham in 1879. Wright also designed a stable to replace an earlier barn. No drawings survive, but Charles E. White, who worked for Wright in the early 1900s, converted the stables to living quarters in 1929. The photograph shows the converted stable, but what remains from Wright's earlier design is unclear.

EDWARD C. WALLER ESTATE, RIVER FOREST, 1899, 1901

In addition to an 1899 remodeling of his friend Edward C. Waller's house, Wright designed a new poultry house and stables for his large estate in 1901. The stables (at left) were clearly in the Prairie mode, with their horizontal massing and trim. The triangular spiked vents look forward to those Wright would use on his own farm buildings at Taliesin in the 1930s. The home (at right) and poultry house were demolished in 1939, and what remained of the stables was destroyed in the early 1970s. Photograph by Philander W. Barclay, 1903. Courtesy the Historical Society of Oak Park and River Forest.

RIVER FOREST GOLF CLUB, RIVER FOREST, 1898, 1901

The rising popularity of golf provided Wright with several commissions over the years, including the River Forest Golf Club,

designed in 1898 and located at what is now Harlem Avenue and Quick Street. In 1901, he added an octagonal lounge with

two fireplaces. The design, with its rustic board-and-batten siding, low, hipped roof, and bands of wood-mullioned windows,

looked distinctly Prairie. When the golf club moved west to a larger property in 1905, the clubhouse was demolished.

Photograph by Philander W. Barclay. Courtesy the Historical Society of Oak Park and River Forest.

River Forest Tennis Club, River Forest, 1905

The River Forest Tennis Club was originally in the same general location as the golf club. After a 1905 fire destroyed an earlier club-house, Wright and fellow members Charles E. White and Vernon S. Watson collaborated on a replacement structure that was largely of Wright's design. When the property was sold to the Cook Country Forest Preserve District in 1920, the building was moved five blocks west to its present location. Watson was responsible for the move and for additions and revisions that negated much of Wright's design. Photograph courtesy Oak Park Public Library, Oak Park, Illinois.

LOST, ALTERED, AND POSSIBLY WRIGHT

E. A. Cummings Real Estate Office, River Forest, 1905

Both the River Forest Tennis and Golf Clubs were built on land provided by real estate broker and developer Edmond A. Cummings. On the south side of the property, facing busy Lake Street, Cummings commissioned Wright in 1905 to design a branch office of his downtown Chicago firm. The small building, whose size was exaggerated by low garden walls extending to the east and west, enclosed a reception area with a fireplace and one private office. It too was a casualty of the sale to the Forest Preserve District and was demolished in 1925. Photograph by Philander W. Barclay, 1903. Courtesy the Historical Society of Oak Park and River Forest.

PEBBLES & BALCH SHOP, OAK PARK, 1907

The Pebbles Company began selling paint and wallpaper in Oak Park as early as 1868. By the time Wright was commissioned to remodel its store on Lake Street in 1907, the business had expanded to include furniture, window treatments, and other decorating items and was headed by the founder's nephew, Frank Pebbles Jr., a friend of the Wright family. His partner until 1908 was Oscar Balch, for whom Wright later designed a house.

The fenestration had a Japanese feel, with its screenlike display and clerestory windows. Pebbles moved his business to a new location in the mid-1930s, and the store was demolished in the 1950s to make way for a larger building. Photographer: Grant Manson. From Henry Russell Hitchcock, *In the Nature of Materials.* Courtesy the Historical Society of Oak Park and River Forest.

LOST, ALTERED, AND POSSIBLY WRIGHT

SCOVILLE PARK FOUNTAIN, OAK PARK, 1909

Now located at the entrance to Scoville Park at the corner of Lake Street and Oak Park Avenue, about one hundred feet

east of the original location, this fountain is a re-creation of a work that has variously been attributed to Wright and to

sculptor Richard Bock (1865–1949). The original was called the Horse Show Fountain and was dedicated on July 24,

1909. This copy was installed in 1969 to mark (incorrectly, since he was born in 1867) Wright's one hundredth birthday.

Bock himself credited Wright with suggesting the opening in the fountain's center, but he states in his memoirs that the rest

of the composition was entirely his own.

SELECTED BIBLIOGRAPHY

Bock, Richard W. *Memoirs of an American Artist, Sculptor: Richard W. Bock.* Edited by Dorathi Bock Pierre. Los Angeles: C. C. Publishing, 1989.

Brooks, H. Allen. *The Prairie School: Frank Lloyd Wright and His Midwest Contemporaries.* New York: W. W. Norton, 1972.

Gill, Brendan. *Many Masks: A Life of Frank Lloyd Wright.* New York: G. P. Putnam's Sons, 1987.

Heinz, Thomas A. *The Vision of Frank Lloyd Wright.* Edison, NJ: Chartwell Books, 2000.

Hitchcock, Henry Russell. *In the Nature of Materials: The Buildings of Frank Lloyd Wright, 1887–1941.* New York: Duell, Sloan & Pearce, 1942.

Levine, Neil. *The Architecture of Frank Lloyd Wright.* Princeton, NJ: Princeton University Press, 1996.

Lind, Carla. *Lost Wright: Frank Lloyd Wright's Vanished Masterpieces.* New York: Simon & Schuster, 1996.

Manson, Grant C. *Frank Lloyd Wright to 1910: The First Golden Age.* New York: Van Nostrand Reinhold, 1958.

McCarter, Robert. *Frank Lloyd Wright.* London: Phaidon Press, 1997.

Pfeiffer, Bruce Brooks, and Futagawa, Yukio. *Frank Lloyd Wright.* 12 vols. Tokyo: A. D. A. Edita, 1984–1988. (Vols. 1–3, *Monograph,* cover the years 1887–1913.)

Purcell, William Gray, Papers. Northwest Architectural Archives. University of Minnesota Libraries, Minneapolis, MN.

Secrest, Meryle. *Frank Lloyd Wright: A Biography.* New York: Alfred A. Knopf, 1992.

Siry, Joseph M. *Unity Temple: Frank Lloyd Wright and Architecture for Liberal Religion.* New York: Cambridge University Press, 1996.

Sprague, Paul E. *Frank Lloyd Wright and Prairie School Architecture in Oak Park.* 5th ed. Oak Park, IL: Oak Park Landmarks Commission, 1986.

Storrer, William Allin. *The Architecture of Frank Lloyd Wright: A Complete Catalog.* 3rd ed. Chicago: University of Chicago Press, 2002. First published 1974 by MIT Press.

Tafel, Edgar. *Apprentice to Genius: Years with Frank Lloyd Wright.* New York: McGraw-Hill, 1979.

Weil, Zarine, ed. *Building a Legacy: The Restoration of Frank Lloyd Wright's Oak Park Home and Studio.* San Francisco: Pomegranate Communications, 2001.

Wright, Frank Lloyd. *An Autobiography.* New York: Horizon Press, 1977.

———. *Frank Lloyd Wright: Ausgeführte Bauten.* Berlin: Ernst Wasmuth, 1911.

———. *Sixty Years of Living Architecture: The Work of Frank Lloyd Wright.* New York: Solomon R. Guggenheim Museum, 1953. Exhibition catalog.

———. *Studies and Executed Buildings of Frank Lloyd Wright (Ausgeführte Bauten und Entwürfe von Frank Lloyd Wright.* A photoreprint of the Berlin edition with an English introduction. Palos Park, IL: Prairie School Press, 1975.

Dear Gerald,
Thanks so much. We're
for Beyond the Score. We're
so sorry its ending – a great
Last for CSO and us.
Marilyn Wechsler and Henry Landy

Dear G –
So many thanks for
your friendship and
enlightenment. You
will be missed –
R (& D)

Grant –
We're so sorry you're
leaving – we'll miss you.
Cat + Goofs

Dear Gerard,
Thank you for sharing
your creativity and expertise
with Chicago. Across the
a friend across the
Pond, Mary Hunt
15-X-16

Frank Lloyd Wright Sites in Oak Park and River Forest

River Forest

1 Waller Gates
Auvergne Place at Lake Street

2 William H. Winslow House
515 Auvergne Place

3 Isabel Roberts House
603 N. Edgewood Place

4 Chauncey Williams House
530 N. Edgewood Place

5 J. Kibben Ingalls House
562 N. Keystone Avenue

6 E. Arthur Davenport House
559 N. Ashland Avenue

7 River Forest Tennis Club
615 N. Lathrop Avenue

Oak Park

8 Walter H. Gale House
1031 W. Chicago Avenue

9 Thomas H. Gale House
1027 W. Chicago Avenue

10 Robert P. Parker House
1019 W. Chicago Avenue

11 Frank Lloyd Wright Home and Studio
951 W. Chicago Avenue

12 Francis J. Woolley House
1030 W. Superior Street

13 William H. Copeland House
400 N. Forest Avenue

14 Nathan G. Moore House
333 N. Forest Avenue

15 Arthur B. Heurtley House
318 N. Forest Avenue

16 Hills-DeCaro House
313 N. Forest Avenue

17 Laura Gale House
6 Elizabeth Court

18 Peter A. Beachy House
238 N. Forest Avenue

19 Frank W. Thomas House
210 N. Forest Avenue

20 Harrison P. Young House
334 N. Kenilworth Avenue

21 Unity Temple
875 W. Lake Street

22 George W. Smith House
404 S. Home Avenue

23 Scoville Park Fountain
Corner of Lake Street and
Oak Park Avenue

24 George W. Furbeck House
223 N. Euclid Avenue

25 Charles E. Roberts Stable
(remodeled by Charles E. White)
317 N. Euclid Avenue

26 Charles E. Roberts House
(interior remodeling)
321 N. Euclid Avenue

27 Edwin H. Cheney House
520 N. East Avenue

28 Harry C. Goodrich House
534 N. East Avenue

29 William E. Martin House
636 N. East Avenue

30 Rollin Furbeck House
515 N. Fair Oaks Avenue

31 William G. Fricke House
540 N. Fair Oaks Avenue

32 Harry S. Adams House
710 W. Augusta Street

33 Oscar B. Balch House
611 N. Kenilworth Avenue

Thomas St

Augusta St

Iowa St

Thatcher Ave

Lathrop Ave

Des Plaines River

Forest Preserve

Canadian National RR

Oak Ave

Edgewood Pl

Keystone Avenue

Forest Avenue

Park Ave

Franklin Ave

Ashland Ave

River Oaks Dr

Auvergne Pl

Central Ave

Hawthorne Ave

Forest Preserve

Linden St

Park Ave

Franklin Ave

Ashland Ave

Washington Blvd

Park Dr.

Thatcher Ave

Vine St

Vine St

Lathrop Ave

Gale Ave

Keystone Ave

Forest Ave

N